DASSAULT RAFALE

The Gallic Squall

HUGH HARKINS

ISBN: 1-903630-92-4
ISBN-13: 978-1-903630-92-1

Dassault Rafale

The Gallic Squall

Centurion Publishing

United Kingdom

ISBN 10: 1-903630-92-4
ISBN 13: 978-1-903630-92-1

This volume first published in 2020

This volume has adopted a quasi-Harvard Manual of Style for referencing. It has, however, not always been possible to adopt a standard referencing format

CONTENTS

INTRODUCTION

The Dassault Rafale, designed to replace a number of legacy aircraft types in French Air Force and Naval aviation service, is a $4^{th}+/4^{th}++$ generation omnirole combat aircraft, which emerged from the French ACX (*Avion de Combat Experimental*) program of the early 1980's. This progressed after France withdrew from the consortium of European partner nations, which went on to develop the Eurofighter Typhoon.

The Rafale design is centred on a comprehensive multi-sensor avionics suite, embracing the concept of sensor fusion to enhance overall mission effectiveness. The integral internal and external sensors and comprehensive array of precision guided weapons enable Rafale to conduct a plethora of operational missions, ranging from air defence, air to surface strike, including nuclear stand-off strike and maritime surface strike, to reconnaissance intelligence gathering.

The volume covers the evolution of the Rafale concept from the early AXC studies that led to the Rafale A technology demonstrator through the succession of serial produced Rafale Standards built or planned – F1to F5. All technical and historical information regarding the aircraft, systems and weapons, have been furnished by the respective designers/developers, as has much of the graphic material, with technical and graphic input from other entities, such as the French *Délégué Général pour l'armament* and respective operators. Certain segments of updated text, where pertinent, are taken from the volumes 'Dassault Rafale, the Gallic Squall' (Harkins, 2004) and 'Eurofighter Typhoon, Storm over Europe' (Harkins, 2013).

1

THE ROAD TO AVION DE COMBAT EXPERIMENTAL

Planning for a 4th (later elevated to 4+/4++) generation tactical combat aircraft for the *Armée de l'Air* (French Air Force) and *Aeronavale* (French Naval Air Arm), which led to the Dassault Rafale, can be traced back to the early to mid-1970's. In this period, a number of western European nations, including France, were pondering their options to obtain next generation tactical combat aircraft for their respective air arms. Some western European nations, notably Denmark, Holland, Norway and The Netherlands, were content to purchase an off the shelf American design – the General Dynamics (later Lockheed Martin) F-16 Fighting Falcon – with licence production being the best that their aircraft manufacturing industries could expect. Others European nations, notably Sweden, West Germany, Italy, the United Kingdom and France, remained steadfast in their determination to design, develop and build their next generation combat aircraft, either indigenously or as part of European collaborative ventures (Harkins, 2013, Harkins, 2004 & Harkins, 1997).

The French ACT 88 (*Avion de Combat Tactique 88*) requirement was aimed at replacement of the SEPECAT (*Societe Europeene de Production de Avion de Ecole de Combat et de' Appuie Tactique*) Jaguar, Dassault Mirage III and Mirage F1 and potentially to supplement and eventually supplant the Dassault Mirage 2000 series, which was in the development stage during the 1970's. The Mirage 2000 series was born as a program to develop a smaller, cheaper, single engine alternative to the Mirage 4000 twin engine tactical combat aircraft developed in concert with the Mirage 2000 and flown in prototype form. Across the English Channel, the British RAF (Royal Air Force) search for a fourth generation tactical combat aircraft was being formulated under AST.396, issued in the early 1970's. This called for a ground attack aircraft with good range-payload and STOVL (Short Take-Off and Vertical Landing) capability to replace the SEPECAT Jaguar and BAC (British Aircraft Corporation), later BAe (British Aerospace), first generation Harrier STOVL ground attack/reconnaissance aircraft fleet (Harkins, 2013, Harkins, 2004 & Harkins, 1997).

Rafale C (foreground) in air defence configuration and Rafale B (background) configured for a stand-off strike mission. Dassault Aviation- K. Tokunaga

During the period of ACT 88 and AST.396, European Air Forces were then absorbing the impact of the outstanding manoeuvrability and multirole capability of the F-16 and Northrop YF-17 Cobra (later evolved into the McDonnell Douglas (now Boeing) F/A-18 Hornet). These American designs were developed to provision the USAF/USN (United States Air Force/United States Navy) with new generation lightweight tactical fighter aircraft. The RAF began revising its fighter requirement to combine the air superiority/interception role with that of ground attack/strike. This resulted in the move from AST.396 to a new target capability under AST.403, which was drawn up around a notional multirole combat aircraft concept. Unlike the Tri-national Panavia

Tornado and French Mirage 2000, then in flight-test, the new combat aircraft would be multirole in practice as well as in name. The Mirage 2000 and Tornado, which was originally labelled the MRCA (Multi-Role Combat Aircraft), were both produced in mission specific variants, including strike and air defence variants (Harkins, 2013, Harkins, 2004 & Harkins, 1997).

Previous page: Dassault Mirage 4000 (top) and Mirage 2000C (bottom). This page top: Mirage 2000D/N incorporated a second cockpit. Bottom: Spanish Air Force Mirage F.1. Dassault/US DoD/Dassault Aviation/Author

The Mirage 2000 was initially procured for the French Air Force in a number of variants – the Mirage 2000B/C for the air defence role, the Mirage 2000D for the ground attack role and the Mirage 2000N for the nuclear strike role. While export variants of the Mirage 2000, based on the Mirage 2000C/B, had a limited multirole functionality, this fell short of true multirole capability of the type envisioned for ACT 88. Only with the introduction of the Mirage 2000-5/-5MK2 (2000-9) variants, in effect a second generation Mirage 2000 series, was Dassault able to claim true multirole capability for the Mirage 2000. Unlike the Tornado and first generation Mirage 2000, the new European 4th generation tactical fighter concept(s) being proposed in the late 1970's/early 1980's would be designed to combine all mission functions within a common airframe with common avionics (Harkins, 2013, Harkins, 2004 & Harkins, 1997).

Even with the new Air Staff Target, the RAF still required a STOVL aircraft design in order to field a viable replacement for its ageing fleet of Harrier GR.3/T.4 ground attack aircraft. However, it was becoming clear that the new 4th generation fighter, like the Jaguar and Tornado before, would most likely be designed and built as a co-operative venture with other European nations. As none of the potential collaborative nations, mainly West Germany and France, required STOVL capability, Britain was put under pressure to drop said STOVL as a capability requirement. This resulted in the British AST.403 being retained to find a replacement for the Jaguar ground attack aircraft, with the RAF's McDonnell Douglas Phantom FG.1/FGR.2 fighter/interceptor fleets now included, but with the Harrier replacement omitted – this would be met by AST.409, which yielded the McDonnell Douglas (later Boeing)/BAe (later BAE Systems) second generation Harrier (Harkins, 2013, Harkins, 2004 & Harkins, 1997).

With the STOVL requirement gone from AST.403, Britain began seriously looking at combining its program with that of West Germany and France under ASR.414. The French *ACT 88* requirement was still aimed primarily at fielding a Jaguar, Mirage IIIE and Mirage F1 replacement. France and Britain were coming into line with similar requirements – replacement for fighter/ground attack fleets – the West German Luftwaffe required a new fighter to replace its McDonnell Douglas (now Boeing) F-4F interceptor and RF-4E Phantom II tactical reconnaissance aircraft fleets (Harkins, 2013, Harkins, 2004 & Harkins, 1997).

From an early stage it was clear that a collaborative European venture would be advantageous from political and economic viewpoints, as this would combine the research and development investment of all three partner nations and the larger production output of a single aircraft design would, in theory, push down unit costs. However, there were many problems to overcome. As noted above, France and Britain both originally required a replacement for ground attack aircraft as both countries were then developing replacements for their respective fighter/interceptor fleets whilst the West German Luftwaffe was focussed on procuring a high agility fighter aircraft to replace its obsolescent F-4 Phantom II fleet. Furthermore, whilst Britain wanted the new aircraft around 1987, France was looking at a 1991 in-service date. Despite these problems the governments of France, Britain and West Germany were publically optimistic that sufficient common ground existed to set up a tri-national study group that would be referred to under the ECA (European Combat Aircraft) label (Harkins, 2013, Harkins, 2004 & Harkins, 1997).

During 1981, the prospective European partner nations continued working on purely national projects. The French ACX spawned a twin-engine, canard-delta concept, which was named Rafale. This early artist impression shows the ACX sporting the original tall vertical tail surface. Dassault Aviation

In 1979, BAe and MBB (Messerschmitt-Bölkow-Blohm) put forward a joint proposal to the British and West German governments for an aircraft design referred to as the ECF (European Combat Fighter). Both governments remained indecisive whilst calling for additional partners to join the collaborative program. In 1980, BAe and MBB joined with Dassault-Breguet of France with the aim of arriving at a design acceptable to all three nations. The partner nations eventually decided on a twin-engine, single seat, canard-delta layout, which, it was considered, offered the best approach to meeting the, at this time, informal mission requirements. However, the design of the aircraft, which was now being referred under the ECA label (noted above) was far from settled, partly due to the three Air Staffs of the respective partner nation's inability to agree on a common operational requirement for the new combat aircraft concept. Throughout 1980 and into 1981, all three countries argued out the technical and political problems, which, combined with France's later insistence on a smaller, lighter aircraft design able to operate from French Navy aircraft carriers, led to the demise of the ECA in 1981 (Harkins, 2013, Harkins, 2004 & Harkins, 1997).

In the early 1980's, BAe was working on canard delta layout designs. The P.110 (1981), featuring twin-vertical tails and lateral engine air intakes, emerged from studies of single and twin engine designs, including the P.106. BAE Systems

During this period, all three partner nations continued work on purely national fighter projects – BAe P.110 (UK), MBB TKF-90 (*Taktisches Kampfflugeuz* 1990) (West Germany) and Dassault-Breguet with its ACX (*Avion de Combat Experimental*) (France), which would eventually evolve into the Dassault Rafale. The P.110, which emerged in 1981, evolved from the BAe single engine, single vertical tail, cranked canard-delta P.106 LCA (Light Combat Aircraft), a study conducted in 1980/1981 for an agile fighter/ground attack aircraft. The P.110 followed the P.106 basic layout, but with a fuselage redesigned to incorporate a duel engine configuration. The TKF-90, which was displayed in mock-up form at the ILA-80 trade show in Hanover, West Germany, was also a canard-delta twin engine fighter design featuring twin vertical tails and a large ventral engine intake complex. A Dornier/Northrop proposal, designated ND-102, which emerged about this time, featured a trapezoidal wing and non-afterburning engines with thrust vector control of engine exhaust. This drawing board design was displayed in model form at the ILA-80 trade exhibition. Aeritalia of Italy was also continuing its own studies into 4th generation tactical fighter aircraft designs (Harkins, 2013, Harkins, 2004 & Harkins, 1997).

In April 1982, the three Panavia Partners that had developed the combined their design studies, leading to the emergence of the Agile Combat Aircraft, which was formerly unveiled at the 1982 Farnborough air show in September of that year. BAE Systems

In April 1982, the Panavia partners that had produced the Tornado – BAe, MBB and Aeritalia – combined design efforts. This led to the emergence of the ACA (Agile Combat Aircraft), unveiled at the 1982 SBAC (Society of British Aerospace Companies) Farnborough trade show in September that year. While remaining in talks with prospective partners, France lost no haste in continuation of her indigenous future fighter design. In June 1982, Dassault-Breguet announced to the French National Assembly that studies for a fighter beyond the Mirage 2000 were well advanced under the guise of the ACX program. At the Farnborough trade show in September 1982, the British government announced that it would provide financial support for a technology demonstrator under the EAP (Experimental Aircraft Program), which would demonstrate technologies for the ACA, with a projected first flight in April 1986. The 1982 Farnborough trade show was also the launch platform for the French ACX technology demonstrator program, which, like the EAP, was scheduled to make its maiden flight in 1986 (Harkins, 2013 & Harkins 2004).

While the three Panavia partner nations pushed on with the Agile Combat Aircraft program, France continued unilateral design studies of her *Avion de Combat Experimental* design. Dassault Aviation

While presenting an ACX progress report to the National Assembly in December 1982, the French Defence Minister invited the ACA partners to participate in the experimental phase of the ACX program. Not unexpectedly, this offer was declined, the ACA partners instead concentrating on their own design concept. France always appeared to be one step ahead of the ACA partners. A contract was signed for the construction of two ACX demonstrators on 13 April 1983. This was well over a month prior to a similar contract, signed on 26 May 1983, by the United Kingdom government, authorising construction of the EAP demonstrator. Along with development of the ACX, engine design house SNECMA, was contracted to develop the M88 turbofan engine to power the new French fighter concept (Harkins, 2013 & Harkins 2004).

Following the decision to proceed with the ACX demonstrator project earlier in the year, Dassault-Breguet exhibited a full-scale mock-up of the concept at the Paris Air Salon in June 1983. This mock-up featured a prominently large single vertical tail surface to address directional stability, and a novel air inlet design – mounted in a semi-ventral position under the wing leading-edge root – to facilitate enhanced air feed efficiency to the engines when the aircraft was flying at high angles of attack. The inlets of the mock-up incorporated movable conical centre-bodies similar to those adopted for the Dassault Mirage family of combat aircraft. The delta type main wing featured compound sweep and straight cropped tips. As was the case with many European tactical combat aircraft concept studies, including the TKF-90 and EAP, the ACX featured close-coupled all-moving canard foreplanes (Harkins, 2013 & Harkins, 2004).

In December 1983, the Chiefs of Staff of France, the United Kingdom, West Germany, Italy and Spain, signed an agreement for an outline ESR (European Staff Requirement) for a new European fighter program, which, around this time, received the designation Future European Fighter Aircraft (FEFA), but was re-designated European Fighter Aircraft (EFA) a short time later. A statement at the meeting specified an agile, twin-engine, single-seat, STOL (Short Take-Off and Landing) fighter design, optimised for BVR (Beyond Visual Range) air to air combat and short range air superiority over the battlefield, whilst incorporating a considerable air to surface capability. In July 1984, the Defence Ministers of the five countries met in Madrid (Spain), reaching an agreement to proceed with the feasibility study, which was scheduled to be completed by the next ministerial meeting in March 1985. The Madrid meeting also outlined the need for a new engine for EFA, which, in its previous incarnations as the ECF and ACA, was planned to be powered by two Turbo Union RB199-67 afterburning turbofan engines, a variant of the RB199 that powered the Panavia Tornado. This was a developed version of the basic engine, able to produce considerably more thrust, estimated at ~9525 kgf (~21,000 lbf.) SNECMA was, at that time, progressing with development of its M88 afterburning turbofan, which it considered the logical choice for any tactical combat aircraft program in which France was a partner. The definitive European Staff Requirement was agreed at a Chiefs of Air Staff meeting in Rome in October 1984 (Harkins, 2013 & Harkins, 2004).

In the decade before the emergence of the ACX, France had developed a variant of the SEPECAT Jaguar as a potential naval strike fighter, this ultimately falling by the wayside. Marine Nationale

The feasibility study threw up many problems with few solutions to be found. The most insurmountable problem appeared to be the French insistence that the fighter aircraft concept should mature as a smaller, lighter design in order that a naval variant could be developed for the *Aeronavale* as a replacements for that services Vought F-8E(FN) Crusader fighter/interceptor and Dassault-Breguet Super Etendard strike fighter fleets. France was looking for an empty weight in the region of 8500 kg, whilst Britain required a design with an empty weight in the region of 11000 kg. In late 1984, EFA empty weight was put at 9500 kg, a clear compromise between the initial French and British weight values. All of the partner nations, with the exception of France, seemed prepared to compromise in order to reach agreement – none of the partner nations other than France stipulated a naval fighter aircraft requirement. The rocky road to divorce got no smoother going into 1985 as the compromises did not go far enough to reduce weight values to align close enough to that required by France (Harkins, 2013, Harkins, 2004 & Harkins, 1997).

In the 1980's, France operated a tactical aircraft fleet of Vought F-8 Crusader fighter interceptor (illustrated starboard), Dassault Etendard IV – reconnaissance – and Dassault Super Etendard strike/attack aircraft (illustrated port). US DoD

France had also demanded design leadership, 46%-50% of total work share, control of the new joint industrial company, which, it required to be based in France, and full control over export sales. Following discussions with the other partner countries, France amended its work share requirement to a still substantial 31%, but retained the demand for design leadership. The French demands proved unacceptable to the remaining partner nations, particularly Britain and West Germany. At an August 1985 meeting in Turin, Italy, the three Panavia partner nations, Britain, West Germany and Italy, withdrew from the negotiations and announced their intention to proceed with a tri-national EFA program. France and Spain were both invited to rejoin the program, although, this would be on the condition that the basic specification of EFA, which by then had a specified empty weight of 9750 kg, was accepted. Spain accepted the offer to rejoin the program in September 1985, but France declined and instead proceeded with her unilateral ACX, which at that time, had an empty weight of 8 tonne (8000 kg) (Harkins, 2013, Harkins, 2004, Harkins, 2004a & Harkins, 1997).

In June 1982, Dassault-Breguet announced to the French National Assembly that studies for a fighter design beyond the Mirage 2000 was well underway under the guise of the Avion de Combat Experimental program. Like the rival British EAP, the ACX was officially launched at the SBAC trade show in September 1982. Dassault Aviation

When construction work commenced on the French ACX demonstrator in 1984, funding cuts had reduced this program to a single unit, the same as the rival EAP – originally three EAP demonstrators were to have been built, one in each of the three Panavia partner nations, but the West German and Italian aircraft were cancelled. By the time of its official rollout at Dassault-Breguet St Cloud plant on 14 December 1985, the ACX had become known as the Dassault Rafale (Squall) A.

Rafale A01 is seen during a change of a General Electric F404 turbofan engine. Dassault Aviation

The Rafale A was of close-coupled canard-delta configuration, with a mid-set compound delta wing incorporating full-span leading-edge slats linked to the full-span trailing-edge elevons. These, along with the all-moving canard foreplanes, which were positioned just forward of the wing leading edge and fuselage junction, were primarily of CFC (Carbon Fibre Composite) construction. Around 50% of the fuselage and the swept vertical tail surface were constructed of CFC, whilst around 35% of airframe weight was of modern construction materials. Rafale A had single main-wheel undercarriage units, which retracted to lay in the fuselage, and a single nose wheel unit. The cockpit, which was covered by a starboard-hinging canopy, accommodated a single pilot on a Martin Baker MK16 zero-zero ejection seat, reclined at an angle of 32°. Basic dimensions included an airframe length of 15.80 m and a wingspan of 11.20 m. The design had a basic empty of 9500 kg – down from an earlier design iteration weight of 10000 kg. When it conducted its maiden flight the Rafale A was 450 kg heavier than the planned series design, then carrying the initial designation Rafale D (Harkins, 2004).

Compared with the 1983 ACX mock-up, the Rafale A01 demonstrator emerged with a vertical tail fin of reduced height and area and a redesigned lower forward fuselage, which now appeared in a quasi 'V' configuration underside, improving air flow to the engines at high angles of attack. As development of the SNECMA M88 turbofan was a long way from flight testing, Rafale A01 was initially to be powered by a pair of GE (General Electric) F404-GE-400 turbofan engines, each rated at ~68.60 kN (~6995 kgf) with afterburner (Harkins, 2004).

The Rafale A demonstrator emerged from the ACX study of the early 1980's. The aircraft is seen during a test flight equipped with MATRA R.550 Magic II air-to-air missile aerodynamic shapes on the wingtip launch rails. Dassault Aviation

The Rafale A demonstrator (top) underwent ground testing and fast taxi trials prior to its maiden flight, conducted on 4 July 1986, just over a month ahead of the British Aerospace EAP (bottom), which conducted its maiden flight on 8 August that year. Like the Rafale A demonstrator, the EAP was with an interim power plant, notably the Turbo Union RB.104E. Dassault Aviation/BAE Systems

Rafale A01 in an almost vertical climb during flight-testing. Dassault Aviation

Although the concerned governments would vehemently deny it, there indeed seemed to be an unofficial race to get the ACX and EAP into the air ahead of each other. For the most part, France was always slightly ahead of her British rival, although this was attributed more to

British political indecision and a strike at BAe Warton than to technical/technological issues. Following its formal rollout the Rafale A, which had received the serial F-ZJRE, was disassembled and transported by road from St Cloud to the Dassault flight test facility at Istres, France. Once reassembled the Rafale A underwent ground testing, including the full spectrum of ground runs, prior to its maiden flight on 4 July 1986, just under a month ahead of the EAP, which had been rolled-out on 16 April 1986 and conducted its maiden flight at Warton on 8 August that year. Dassault chief test pilot, Guy-Maurouard, was at the controls of the Rafale A for the one hour maiden flight, during which the aircraft attained a maximum speed of Mach 1.3, an altitude of ~10971 m and manoeuvred at loads up to 5 g. Over the next few days the flight envelope was opened up and the aircraft demonstrated a speed of Mach 1.8 during its first week of flight test. Rafale A01 had conducted enough flying hours to allow the aircraft to be displayed at the 1986 SBAC show at Farnborough, where it made its public debut on 31 August that year (Harkins, 2013, Harkins, 2004 & Harkins, 1997).

Following the public debut at Farnborough, the flight envelope of Rafale A01 was progressively opened, allowing the potential of the aircraft to be demonstrated. During the period 18-28 November 1986, Rafale A01 was put through an initial operational evaluation conducted at CEV (*Centre d'Essais en Vol*) Istres. Six pilots from Dassault-Breguet, the French Air Force and *Aeronavale* conducted the evaluation, which included assessing the Rafale A flight characteristics on the approach to an aircraft carrier deck – in this instance employing a virtual deck painted on a runway at Istres (Harkins, 2004).

Rafale A01 during practice landing approach. Note small airbrakes at the base of the vertical tail, a system omitted from serial aircraft. Dassault Aviation

Rafale A01 in flight, illustrating the fuselage carriage of MICA medium range air to air missile aerodynamic shapes. Dassault Aviation-F. Robineau

By completion of phase 1 testing in January 1987, Rafale A01 had flown 90 times, following which the aircraft entered overhaul and was equipped with additional instrumentation required for phase 2. Phase 2, conducted from 26 February 1987, saw the aircraft configured with several external stores combinations that included various inert flight rated aerodynamic missiles shapes and 2000 litre external fuel tanks. A major milestone was reached on 4 March 1987 when the aircraft demonstrated a speed of Mach 2 whilst flying at an altitude of 13000 m. This was in excess of the Mach 1.8 stipulated under the ACT 88 requirement (Harkins, 2004).

Following on from the Istres evaluation, Rafale A01 would be further utilised in the development of the planned naval Rafale M (Marine), despite having no naval specific equipment, such as an arrestor hook. Commencing early 1987, Rafale A01 conducted a number of approaches to the virtual aircraft carrier deck painted on a runway at Nimes-Garons naval air station – chief project pilot for development of the naval variant was Yves Kerhervé. This series of tests was followed by a number of practice approaches to the French Navy aircraft carrier FNS (French Naval Ship) *Clemenceau* on 30 April 1987, which revealed that the

Rafale A possessed excellent approach qualities. A further series of approach trials was accomplished on the aircraft carrier FNS *Foch*, with 85 approaches being conducted between 4 and 8 July 1988. Rafale A01 successfully demonstrated approaches at various angles of attack, crossing the *Foch's* stern at speeds of 222 km/h (~120 knots), a modest reduction over the Super Etendard then in service with the *Aeronavale* (Harkins, 2004).

Rafale A01 was publically demonstrated at the 1987 Paris Air Salon in June that year. During the winter of 1987/1988, test-flights to measure the radar cross section and infrared signature of Rafale A01 were conducted. During the course of 13 flights the radar signature was assessed while the aircraft was configured in several external load configurations. This included MATRA R.550 Magic II air to air missile aerodynamic shapes on an air combat mission profile and a low-level mission profile configured with two 2000 litre external fuel tanks. During external load tests Rafale A01 was also flown in an air combat configuration equipped with two wingtip mounted Magic II and four MATRA MICA aerodynamic shapes on the fuselage pylons (one on the forward fuselage centre station, one on the rear fuselage centre station and two on the rear fuselage shoulder stations). From April 1989, Rafale A01 was involved in trials of the digital flight control system and optical fibre transmission, which ended on 12 July 1989 when the aircraft was grounded for modifications – 460 flights in 430 hours 50 minutes had been flown up to that date. By then Rafale A01 had demonstrated a 32° angle of attack, a minimum controlled flight speed of 148 km/h, a maximum speed at upper altitude of Mach 2 and a maximum speed at low altitude of 1390 km/h (~751 knots) (Harkins, 2004).

The main modification to Rafale A01 was the replacement of the port F404-GE-400 turbofan engine with a development SNECMA M88-2 afterburning turbofan engine rated at ~73.5 kN (~7495 kgf) thrust (this was the engine under development for the ACT (Rafale D). Following installation of the M88-2, Rafale A01 resumed flight test on 27 February 1990, becoming the first aircraft to fly with an M88 engine installed. Between 6 and 9 March 1990, Rafale A01 underwent trials at the CEV, following which the aircraft was handed over to SNECMA for intensive trials of the M88 engine. The aircraft conducted its 856th and final flight on 24 January 1994, leading a formation of all five flying Rafale demonstrator/prototypes – A01, C01, B01, M01 & M02 – following which it was grounded, leaving the flight test development program to the four Rafale development/prototype aircraft. Rafale A01 was later installed on a pole for display at Istres, France (Harkins, 2004).

Dassault Rafale A01 specification – data furnished by Dassault Aviation

Type: Single seat multi-role combat aircraft technology demonstrator
Power plant: two F404-GE-400 afterburning turbofan engines, each rated at ~6995 kgf)-7257 kgf. A single SNECMA M88-2 development engine replaced one of the F404 for flights commencing in 1990.
Dimensions: wing span 11.20 m (~36 ft. 8.9 in); wing area ~47.00 m^2 (~505.92 sq. ft.); aspect ratio 2.03; length 15.80 m (~51 ft. 10 in)
Weights: Empty 9500 kg (~20,944 lb.), combat take-off 1400 kg (~30865 lb.).
Maximum speed, clean configuration: Mach 2
g loads: -3.2 to +9
Crew: One

Rafale A01. Dassault Aviation

Rafale A01 (top), Rafale A01 leading the Mirage 4000 prototype (centre) and the Rafale A01 demonstrator with an M88-2 turbofan engine installed (bottom) – flew in this configuration on 27 February 1990. Dassault Aviation

2

PROTOTYPE TO SERIAL PRODUCTION

The Rafale program was implemented through the combined efforts of Dassault Aviation, the French DGA (*Délégué Général pour l'armament*/General Delegate for Armament), FAF (French Air Force) and *Aeronavale* (French naval air arm) domestic recipients and some 500 industry partners (Dassault, 2020). The Rafale B/C/M prototypes that followed the Rafale A technology demonstrator were smaller and lighter than their predecessor. In 1986, preliminary data suggested the serial Rafale B/C (formerly Rafale D) would span 10.00 m; length, 14.8 m; wing area, 44 m^2 and empty weight, under 9 tonnes, increasing to 9.5 tonnes for the Rafale M. On 14 February 1987, the French government authorised, in principle, development of Rafale to meet a new generation tactical combat aircraft requirement for the FAF/*Aeronavale*. This was based on prior acquired data analysis for an operational design based on technology demonstrated in the Rafale A (Harkins, 2004).

The FAF/*Aeronavale* released a joint requirement for launch of the Rafale development program. This called for an omnirole platform to replace no less than seven French domestic legacy aircraft designs. Replacement of such a wide range of aircraft types by a single platform required design of an air vehicle capable of conducting all legacy aircraft associated roles – air defence, reconnaissance/intelligence gathering, nuclear deterrence (nuclear strike) and air to surface attack/strike (over sea/land). This later role could be broken down to a number of sub-roles – close air support of ground forces, interdiction/strike against targets behind an area of ground operations, or in the absence of ground operations and anti-ship strike (Dassault, 2020).

Rafale C (foreground) and Rafale B (background) of the French Air Force.
Dassault Aviation

The joint requirement release resulted in the 8 April 1987 formation of the industrial group ACE (*Avion de Combat European*) International that was made-up of Dassault-Breguet (now Dassault Aviation), SNECMA (now part of Safran) and Thomson-CSF (now Thales). ACE International attempted, in vain, to interest other European nations in the prospect of joining the group to produce a European combat aircraft (Harkins, 2004).

From early 1987, the postulated serial production land based ACT (*Avion de Combat Tactique*) was known as the Rafale D (Discreet) and the naval variant was known as the Rafale M (Marine). The Rafale D designation had been applied after the DGA stipulated that the design incorporate increased low observable (so called stealth) characteristics. As was the case with the EFA (European Fighter Aircraft) – later Eurofighter Typhoon – it was not possible to turn the Rafale into a low observable design in the class of the Lockheed Martin F-22 (serial evolution of the YF-22 technology demonstrator for service with the United States Air Force) without embarking upon a complete redesign, therefore, emphasis was placed on reducing radar signature where it was practicable to do so without compromising overall platform capability. This included redesigning the vertical tail surface and fuselage junction box, employing radar absorbent coatings on airframe structure and cockpit canopy. In early 1988, the ACE industrial group revealed some details of its low observable work in regard to reduced radar reflectivity of the M88 engine face – among the changes was a redesigned front fuselage (Harkins, 2004).

Rafale A01 conducted its 856th and final flight on 24 January 1994, leading a formation of Rafale C01, M01, M02 and B01. Dassault Aviation

Once the basic design of the aircraft had been finalised, Rafale D received new designations, Rafale B for the two-seat variant and Rafale C for the single-seat variant. The latter designation had previously been informally applied to an informally proposed single-engine variant during 1986/87 – this was not actively promoted by Dassault and fell by the wayside. The Rafale M was not affected by these designation changes (Harkins, 2004).

The French government included funding for the Rafale program in the five-year defence plan announced in mid-1987, with full-scale development authorised in January 1988. On 21 April 1988, the French government and the ACE industry group signed contract W15, formally launching FSD (Full-Scale Development) of the Rafale program. Details of the contract included completion of design definition by 1 July 1988 and a planned maiden flight for the prototype by 1 October 1990 – only a single two-seat (later changed to a single-seat aircraft, Rafale C01) development prototype was covered by the FSD contract, with options for a further four, including two naval Rafale M's. The single Rafale B two-seat prototype was ordered on 19 July 1989, along with the first naval prototype, M01. The second naval prototype, M02, was ordered on 4 July 1990. The fifth prototype option, apparently for a Rafale C, C02, was not taken up to reduce development costs (Harkins, 2004).

Rafale C01, the first of four development (prototypes), conducted its maiden flight on 19 May 1990. Dassault Aviation

Towards the end of 1991, the FAF was indecisive as to what configuration the main Rafale variant should be and commenced an active reconsideration of its approach on arriving at the best solution for its Rafale fleet composition. The original requirement was for 225 single-seat Rafale C and 25 duel control twin-seat Rafale B operational conversion trainers. The FAF now considered changing the bulk of its planned procurement to the two-seat Rafale B in order that a dedicated weapons system operator could be carried. This was born of experience gained during the 1991 Gulf War, which indicated that workload could be high for a single crew member on strike missions. The French Navy, meanwhile, remained committed to taking delivery of the Rafale M, with deliveries, originally scheduled for 1 July 1996, now extended to 1998. In late May 1992, it was, not unexpectedly, announced that the FAF was altering its planned Rafale fleet acquisition to include the two-seat Rafale B as the predominant variant, optimised for the strike/attack mission. Rafale B/C deliveries were scheduled to commence in the period 1998-2000, the delay then being attributed to the program reorganisation following the decision to produce the Rafale B as the predominant variant. In late 1992, the revised FAF requirement for Rafale was formally confirmed as 140 two-seat Rafale B and 94 single seat Rafale C, for a combined total acquisition of 234. This was a unit reduction of 16 from the original requirement for 250, primarily attributed to offsetting increased costs associated with the move to the more expensive, in terms of unit costs, Rafale B (Harkins, 2004).

Page 27-28: Rafale C01, resplendent it an overall black livery, during flight test over the French coast/littoral waters. Dassault Aviation

Rafale C01 banks in a climb over a water surface during flight test. By the time the aircraft retired from flight operations at the end of its ultimate flight on 11 December 2003, a total of 1559 flight hours had been attained in 1287 flights, the last of which involved engine start-ups. Dassault Aviation

The single Rafale C prototype, C01, over a sea surface. Dassault Aviation

Prior to its official rollout, the first prototype Rafale, C01, which had been ordered in April 1988, underwent initial airframe assembly and system tests at Dassault St Cloud test facility where it was formally rolled-out on 29 October 1990. Following the ceremony, the aircraft was moved back into the plant to be disassembled for road transport to Istres two days later, where it was reassembled in readiness for its maiden flight, originally scheduled for February/March 1991. Following some delays, the maiden flight of C01, now carrying the French serial F-ZWVR, was conducted from Istres on 19 May 1991 (pilot, Dassault test pilot Guy Maurouard). This was not only the maiden flight of the Rafale C, but the first flight of a Rafale powered by two M88 engines (when Rafale C01 conducted its maiden flight, Rafale A01 had already flown 73 test flights with an M88 installed in the port engine bay). During the course of C01's maiden flight the aircraft attained an altitude of 10,980 m and a maximum speed of Mach 1.2 indicated air speed, apparently without the use of afterburner (Harkins, 2004).

Rafale M01 conducted its maiden flight on 13 December 1991. Dassault Aviation

On 13 December 1991, the prototype Rafale M, M01, conducted its maiden flight from Istres (pilot, Dassault test pilot Yves Kerhervé.). During the flight, M01 attained an altitude of 12800 m and a speed of Mach 1.4 – C01 had, by this date, conducted around 50 test flights. M01 was followed by a non-flight rated static test airframe, which was utilised for structural/fatigue testing from late 1991 (Harkins, 2004).

The Rafale M prototype, M01, at Farnborough in September 1996 (top) and at Le Bourget Paris (bottom). Author

In the period 15-26 June 1992, Rafale C01 underwent its first service evaluation at Istres. That same month, M01 was prepared for transport to the USA by sea for the first of four planned series of naval catapult/arrestor and aircraft carrier trials at NAS (Naval Air Station) Lakehurst, New Jersey, scheduled for July-August 1992. Fifty eight arrested landings were conducted in fifteen test periods during this phase, which was completed in September 1992. M01 returned to the USA for a catapult launch test phase at NAS Patuxent River, Maryland, Virginia – this test period, conducted in January and February 1993, accomplished 28 ground based catapult launches and 68 arrested landings. The catapult/arrestor trials in the USA prepared the ground for Rafale M01 trials aboard the FNS (French Naval Ship) *Foch*, which commenced when the aircraft landed aboard the aircraft carrier, cruising in the Mediterranean Sea, on 19 April 1993. M01 conducted around 30 takes-offs from the *Foch*, utilising the vessels temporary 1.5° ski-jump located on the bow to assist the generation of lift at the conclusion of the take-off run (Harkins, 2004).

Rafale M01 landing at the Farnborough International trade exhibition in September 1996, with stencilling on the vertical tail to denote that it was the programs 3112th flight. Author

Top: Rafale B01 maiden flight on 30 April 1993. Above: Rafale B01 during stores carriage trials. Dassault Aviation

The two-seat Rafale prototype, B01, conducted a 70 minute maiden flight on 30 April 1993 – the aircraft attained an altitude of 12182 m and a speed of Mach 1.3. B01 would be integrated into the flight development program, being the first Rafale to be equipped with a functional ESA (Electronically Scanned Array) RBE2 radar complex and SPECTRA (Self-Protection Equipment to Counter Threats for Rafale Aircraft – *Systéme de Protection et d'Evitement des Conduites de Tire dee Rafale*) defensive aids complex (Harkins, 2004).

Previous page: Rafale B (top) introduced a second cockpit section not present in the Rafale C or the Rafale M (bottom). This page: Rafale B01 landing at the Farnborough International trade exhibition in 1998. Author

Top: Rafale B01 with a range of projected stores options alongside the aircraft. Bottom: Rafale M02 during testing in the anechoic chamber to measure the electromagnetic signature of the weapon system and measurements of the radar cross section. Author/Dassault Aviation

Rafale M02 conducted its maiden flight from Istres on 8 November 1993 – the aircraft attained an altitude of 13700 m and a speed of Mach 1.3. On the date of M02's maiden flight, M01 commenced a third series of trials in the USA. This period of trials, which ended on 16 December 1993, included some 60 take-off and arrested landings at NAS Lakehurst with the aircraft several stores configurations. Rafale M01 and M02 conducted a joint program of testing aboard the FNS *Foch* between 25 January 1994 and 5 March 1994. The fourth carrier suitability campaign was conducted on the *Foch* during September 1995, and the fourth and final land-based carrier suitability campaign was conducted in the USA during the period October-December 1995. Further development testing of the Rafale M continued through 1999, Rafale M01, for the first time, landing aboard the French Navy nuclear powered aircraft carrier FNS *Charles de Gaulle* on 6 July that year. The first Rafale steam catapult take-off from the *Charles de Gaulle* took place the following day, 7 July. This was followed by at least a further 14 sorties from the vessel, at take-off weights of between 12 and 18 tonnes, up to 22 July 1999 (Harkins, 2004).

The second Rafale M development aircraft, M02 at Le Bourget, Paris. Author

Rafale M02 at Le Bourget airport, Paris. Author

Rafale M prototypes during early aircraft carrier trials on the FNS *Foch*.
Dassault Aviation

Page 41-42: Models of the Rafale B, M, M (with Exocet) and C. Author

The first serial produced Rafale, B301, was one of only a few F1 Standard Rafale intended for the French Air Force (employed on development tasks). The aircraft is here on its maiden flight on 24 November 1998. Dassault Aviation

On 26 March 1993, a single Rafale M and a single Rafale B serial production aircraft were ordered by the French DGA. In the first half of 1994, a second production order was placed for two Rafale M and a single Rafale B. A third order was placed in summer 1995, for a single Rafale B for the FAF and seven Rafale M for the *Aeronavale*. These limited production contracts were brought about through a combination of funding problems and indecision as to the way forward in regard to overall numbers of the respective variants to be procured (Harkins, 2004).

As noted above, originally the FAF had committed to ordering 250 serial Rafale, 25 of which would be two-seat operational conversion trainers, with the balance consisting of single-seat multi-role fighters to replace the few remaining Dassault Mirage III/5, Mirage F1 and to supplement and eventually supplant the Dassault Mirage 2000. Following a reassessment of its needs based on operational experience, the FAF had changed its requirement to cover 94 Rafale C and 140 Rafale B (Harkins, 2004). The *Aeronavale* had an original requirement for 86 Rafale M that were to replace that services obsolescent Vought F-8 Crusader interceptor/fighter and Dassault Super Etendard strike fighter fleets. It was originally planned for initial serial deliveries to the *Aeronavale* to commence in 1996, with 14 Rafale M to be delivered by 1998 to reform Flotilla 12F. This unit was then to embark on the new nuclear powered aircraft carrier FNS *Charles de Gaulle,* which was then scheduled to commission in 1998. By mid to late 1993, Rafale planned service entry with the FAF had been delayed until 1999. At the same time, it was revealed that the *Aeronavale* now planned to receive perhaps in excess of 10 Rafale M to a reduced capability Standard prior to 1999, followed by the next Standard release (this commenced flight test in 1995) featuring full capability in air to air and air to surface roles (Harkins, 2004).

The first series produced Rafale, B301, was employed in development of the F2 Standard Rafale, clearing the way for introduction to service with the French Air Force in 2006. Dassault Aviation

In the event, France ordered four major serial batches (the first, an amalgamation of the previous small scale orders) of Rafale aircraft, numbering 13, 48, 59 and 60, for the FAF and Navy. This is broken down to 63 two-seat Rafale B and 69 single-seat Rafale C for the FAF and 48 Rafale M for the French Navy – 180 in total (Dassault, 2020). In recent years the Rafale program has been boosted through three significant export orders: Qatar and Egypt both ordered 24 Rafale (the Egyptian order is broken down to 16 two-seat and eight single seat aircraft) whilst India ordered 36 in 2015 (Dassault, 2020). In August 2020, Greece was on the cusp of ordering a batch of 18 Rafale fighters. A two-seat naval variant – Rafale N (previously BM), which emerged in summer 2000, did not advance to production (Harkins, 2004).

F1 STANDARD – Rafale was to be released for service in incremental Standards (each with a corresponding increase in capability over their forbear) as technologies became available. Four Standards have been defined – F1 to F4 with a further Standard, F5, under study. As production plans progressed, numerous changes were implemented and then further altered before it was finally settled on producing the initial ten serial Rafale M for the *Aeronavale* to F1 Standard, along with three Rafale for the FAF. To this end, F1 Standard was the first service variant – the F1 Standard Rafale M was declared operational in French Naval service in 2004 (Dassault, 2020).

The first serial Rafale, B301, was officially presented to the French defence minister at the Merignac plant on 4 December 1998, following which it was incorporated into the development program at Istres. B301 was apparently transferred to the CEAM (*Centre d'Expérimentation Aérienne Militaire*/French Test and Evaluation Unit) at Mont-de-Marsan, and was incorporated into the Rafale F2 and F3 Standard development efforts. Between 26 June and 10 July 1999, Rafale B301 deployed to Al Dhafra air base in the UAE (United Arab Emirates) to conduct hot climatic – high temperatures and conditions of humidity – testing (Dassault, 2020).

The first series produced Rafale, B301. Dassault Aviation

Following its maiden flight, the first series produced Rafale M, M1, embarked upon a brief flight expansion test series, ending with the formal delivery of the aircraft in late 1999. Rafale M1 was then based at the Istres flight test center, participating in the final stages of F1 Standard qualification prior to incorporation into the F2 Standard development effort. Dassault-F Robineau

The F1 Standard Rafale M, which, under late 1990's planning, were to be delivered between 1999 and 2002, were cleared for the air combat role armed with medium range MICA EM active-radar guided and short-range R.550 Magic II infrared guided air to air missiles. The F1 Standard ESA RBE2 radar was cleared for the air to air mission and the aircraft was equipped with the SPECTRA self-defence suite (Harkins, 2004).

The first serial produced Rafale M, M1, had conducted an 80 minute maiden flight at Bordeaux-Merignac on 7 July 1999 (pilot, Dassault test pilot Philippe Deleume), during which the aircraft attained an altitude of 15240 m and a speed of Mach 1.2. The previous day, the preliminary trials were conducted with M01 from the FNS *Charles de Gaulle* (noted above). M1 was incorporated into the development/trials program and would be involved in clearance of the F1 and F2 Standards, operating from Dassault Istres facility alongside Rafale B301 and the third serial Rafale, which joined them before the end of 2000 (Harkins, 2004).

Top: Rafale M1 was retained by Dassault to participate in development of the F2 Standard, delivered from 2004. Bottom: The second series produced Rafale M, M2 – the first Rafale to be delivered for service with Flotilla 12F at **Landivisiau** – is shown with F1 Standard missile armament of **MICA EM** and **Magic II air to air missiles.** Marine Nationale

Rafale M2. Marine Nationale

The French Navy formally accepted two Rafale M in a ceremony held at Landivisiau in December 2000 and Flotilla 12F officially stood-up at the air station as the first Rafale squadron (in a training capacity) on 18 May 2001. In support of the Anglo-American operation against Afghanistan, which commenced in October 2001, other nations contributed forces to support the coalition effort against the Afghan Taliban. This included a French contingent, the composition of which included the aircraft carrier FNS *Charles de Gaulle*, which left port on 1 December 2001 on a cruise that would take it to the Indian Ocean and Gulf of Oman. As well as its complement of Dassault Super Etendard *Modernise* strike fighters, the carrier had onboard Rafale M2 and M3 of 12F, which was not yet operational. In February 2002, Rafale M4, M5 and M6 flew out to join M2 and M3 aboard the carrier. These five aircraft were joined by M7 and M8, which landed on the carrier on 10 March 2002, following flight, in excess of 5000 km, from Istres in southern France. Rafale M's of 12F were involved in training operations only (Harkins, 2004).

The last two F1 Standard Rafale M, M9 and M10, were delivered in summer 2002. Toward the end of that year, Rafale M's participated in a three week trial campaign aboard the *Charles de Gaulle* in order to validate a number of external load configurations at heavy weight for the planned F2 and F3 Standard Rafale. During this test period, Rafale M1 – retained by Dassault for development of the F2 Standard – was launched from the carrier deck at a weight of 21.4 tonnes (~21400 kg) carrying a SCALP EG subsonic air launched cruise missile on the fuselage centre station, a pair of 2000 litre external fuel tanks on the inboard wing stations and four MICA air to air missiles – two each on the wingtip and rear fuselage shoulder stations. In another test series, the aircraft landed on the aircraft carrier deck at a weight of 15.7 tonnes (~15700 kg) carrying six AASM (*Armament Air Sol Modulaire*) 250 kg class guided munitions and two empty 2000 litre external fuel tanks. This series of test flights demonstrated the Rafale M stores bring back capability, negating the need to jettison munitions into the sea before being recovered to the aircraft carrier deck (Harkins, 2004).

Further trials and training was conducted over the next few years, paving the way for the Rafale M to be officially inducted into operational service with 12F at Landivisiau on 25 June 2004 (Harkins, 2004). The *Charles de Gaulle* 6 test campaign was conducted in December 2005, integrated with the F3 Standard development, whilst continuing the push toward full commissioning of the F2 Standard Rafale (Dassault AR, 2005).

Above: Rafale M3 was the third F1 Standard serial Rafale for the French Navy.
Marine Nationale

The first series produced Rafale C, C101, during flight-test. Dassault Aviation-F. Robineau

F2 STANDARD – Following the thirteen F1 Standard serial Rafale, the second major production batch consisted of 48 aircraft, ordered in 1999 – 15 for the *Aeronavale* and 23 for the FAF – to be delivered to a Standard that would emerge as F2. The 'F' Standard release approach called for deliveries of F2 Standard Rafale from 2004, followed by the increased capability F3 Standard from 2008. Whilst the F1 Standard was released with a reduced capability air to air functionality only, the F2 Standard, which entered service with the FAF in 2006, was the first to provide omnirole functionality through adding air to ground capability (Dassault, 2020).

Full definition of the F2 standard had commenced in January 1999 and continued into autumn that year. The full development contract was awarded and finalised in the 2000/2001 timeframe, paving the way for the development/trials Rafale fleet to progress in clearing this Standard for service. The first serial single-seat Rafale for the FAF, C101 – this was the first serial Rafale equipped with F2 Standard avionics – conducted its 1 hour 15 minute maiden flight from Mérignac, France, on 16 April 2003 (pilot, Frederic Lascourreges). C101 was heavily involved in the F2 Standard clearance, which included introduction of the enhanced air to air capability, as well as introducing air to surface capabilities (Harkins, 2004).

The main features of the F2 Standard included the enhanced Modular Data Processing Unit (trialled on Rafale B301 and M02 prior to installation in Rafale C101), introduction of the FSO (Front Sector Optronics) passive detection and tracking system), Link-16 data-link capability, enhanced SPECTRA functionality and air to ground modes for the ESA RBE2 radar. F2 Standard further enhanced air to air capability through addition of the MICA IR (Infrared) and introduced air to ground capabilities through integration of air to ground weapons – SCALP EG and AASM precision guided munition (Dassault, 2020, Dassault AR, 2006 & Harkins, 2004).

The first Rafale C was delivered to the FAF on 3 June 2005 (Dassault AR, 2005). The interim Rafale F2.1 Standard, development of which was initiated in January 2001, was qualified on 22 December 2005, and the full F2 Standard was qualified during 2006 (Dassault AR, 2006).

F2 Standard Rafale, M18, deck approach practice on a USN aircraft carrier.
US Navy

F3 STANDARD – The F3 Standard added maritime strike, armed with AM 39 Exocet, airborne reconnaissance/intelligence gathering, equipped with AREOS (Airborne Reconnaissance Observation System) pod system and nuclear strike, armed with ASMPA (*Air-Sol Moyenne Portée Amélioré*), to the Rafale mission capability (Dassault, 2020).

F3 Standard Rafael added maritime strike, armed with AM 39 Exocet air launched subsonic anti-ship cruise missile (top) and stand-off nuclear strike, armed with the MBDA ASMPA air launched supersonic medium range missile (bottom), to the mission roles. Dassault Aviation

In 2006, Dassault had committed to finalisation of the F3 Standard, which commenced flight test in May that year. The *Charles de Gaulle* 7 test campaign was conducted from 4-19 June 2007 to clear F3 Standard stores – AM 39 Exocet and ASMPA air to surface missiles and the AREOS (formerly Recco NG) reconnaissance pod system – for operations with Rafale M. The F3 Standard Rafale conducted launches of AM 39 and ASMPA (Dassault AR, 2007) by mid-2008. The F3 Standard was qualified for service on 2 July 2008, the first F3 Standard Rafale being allocated to the CEAM that summer (Dassault, 2020). The first 3T series produced Rafale was delivered in September 2008, with deliveries of the F3 Standard to Mont-de-Marsan commencing that same month (Dassault AR, 2008).

F2 & F3 Standard Rafale deliveries had facilitated the formation of a number of FAF/*Aeronavale* squadrons. EC (Escadron de Chasse) 1/7 'Provence' commissioned as the first FAF Rafale squadron at Saint Dizier 113 air base on 27 June 2006 (Dassault AR, 2006). EC 1/91 'Gascogne' reformed at Saint Dizier as the second FAF Rafale squadron on 29 March 2009, followed in October the following year by formation of ETR 2/92. This latter unit was designated as a joint French Air Force/French Navy Rafale training squadron. In November 2010, EC 3/30 'Lorraine' re-formed as a FAF Rafale squadron based at Al Dhafra in the UAE (United Arab Emirates). The fourth FAF squadron to be equipped with Rafale was EC 2/30 'Normandie-Niemen, which reformed at Mont-de-Marsan in June 2012 – 11F had reformed as an *Aeronavale* Rafale squadron, following conversion from the Super Etendard at Landivisiau, the previous year (Dassault, 2020).

SIMULATOR – Reception was accomplished in 2007 with the Rafale F2 simulation centre located at Saint-Dizier, with delivery of a simulator by SOGITEC Industries of France. Inauguration of the simulator centre took place on 24 January 2008. A Rafale F2 simulator was inaugurated at Landivisiau on 9 January 2009. The Rafale CSR simulator at Saint Dizier was updated to F3 Standard in 2012 (Dassault AR, 2012, Dassault AR, 2009, Dassault AR, 2008 & Dassault AR, 2007).

New capabilities would continue to be added under the Rafale F3.2 (later designated F3-04T) Standard. This introduced a number of enhancements: the FSO-IT (enhanced FSO), modern DDM NG missile warning system and AESA (Active Electronically Scanned Array) for the RBE2 radar (Dassault, 2020 & Dassault AR, 2012). In 2012, the F3-04T Standard Rafale received qualification. Rafale F3-04T C137 was delivered in October 2012 – the first Rafale to delivered from the production line equipped with the AESA (Dassault AR, 2012).

F1/2 to F3 UPDATE – In 2010, Dassault completed the F2 Standard retrofits to F3 Standard (Dassault AR, 2010). Toward the mid-2010's, a program was initiated for the more complex update of the ten F1 Standard Rafale M to F3 Standard, with the first three redelivered to F3 Standard in 2014 (Dassault AR, 2014). A further two F1 Standard Rafale, updated to F3 Standard, were delivered to the French Navy in 2016 (Dassault AR, 2016). A further three F1 Standard Rafale, updated to F3 Standard, were delivered in 2017 (Dassault AR, 2017) and the final two F1 Standard Rafale M were updated to F3 Standard and redelivered in 2018 (Dassault AR, 2018).

F1 Standard Rafale M8 in 2007. From 2014, the F1 Standard Rafale M were updated to F3 Standard. USN

F3-R – The F3-R Standard was intended to provide improvements to areas identified as requiring such during operations, including systems and sensors (Dassault AR, 2013). A contract was issued by the French government in December 2012, covering update of collective F3 Standard Rafale to F3-R Standard (Dassault AR, 2012) and development commenced in 2014 (Dassault AR, 2017). In 2016, the F3-R was scheduled for qualification and delivery of this Standard in 2018 and 2019 respectively. To meet this schedule the first integration flight of a Rafale with the TALIOS new generation targeting and reconnaissance pod (planned for introduction with F3-R) was conducted in 2016. Other F3-R Standard capability enhancements included integration of the Meteor extended range air to air missile – the final validation launch of a Meteor was conducted in 2017 – and a new variant of the AASM

HAMMER (Highly Agile Modular Munition Extended Range) (Dassault AR, 2016 & (Dassault AR, 2017). Qualification of the F3-R Standard was achieved on 31 October 2018 (Dassault AR, 2018) and an F3-R Standard aircraft was formally delivered that year (Dassault AR, 2019).

Rafale F3-R carrying Meteor air to air missiles on the rear fuselage shoulder stations and a TALIOS pod on the starboard forward shoulder station.
Dassault Aviation-A. Pecchi

F4 STANDARD – The F4 Standard pre-development was formally launched with a French Government announcement of intention to proceed. A reaffirmation of an intent to purchase a total of 225 Rafale stopped short of ordering the expected fifth Rafale production batch (Dassault AR, 2016). Development of the F4 Standard was launched by the French Government with notification of the risk reduction phase toward the end of 2017, and funding was incorporated into the 2019 to 2025 military spending bill – a fifth production batch covering 30 aircraft was expected during this period (Dassault AR, 2017). The full-scale development contract for the F4 Standard was awarded during the French Minister of armed forces visit to Mérignac on 14 January 2019 (Dassault AR, 2018).

The F4 Standard enhancements would improve connectivity – enhancing networked combat capabilities (incorporation of new satellite communications, new communication server, intra-patrol connections and new software, enhancing radio communications – improvements to aircraft survivability and enhanced overall operational capabilities and platform reliability. The radar and FSO sensor suite was to be updated and capability enhanced through addition of a helmet mounted sight and an automatic anti-collision system was to be introduced. New weapons planned for incorporation into the F4 Standard included MICA NG (Next Generation) and laser guided 1000 kg AASM HAMMER. A new electronic engine control unit was to be introduced and measures incorporated to enhance maintenance, including adopting so called artificial intelligence for diagnostics and failure prediction. F4 Standard validation was scheduled for 2024, with some capability expected to be available from 2022 (Dassault AR, 2018 & Dassault AR, 2019).

In August 2020, work on the F4 Standard was underway utilising Rafale M38 under project management of the DGA. DGA

French domestic commitments in 2020 stood at 225 Rafale aircraft (down on a previous requirement for 300), 180 of which had been ordered (Dassault, 2020). Toward the end of 2010, the FAF had received some 62 Rafale – 38 B and 24 C – whilst the French Navy had taken delivery of 31 Rafale M. By this time, around 100 of the 180 Rafale ordered by the DGA had been delivered (Dassault, 2020) for service or to test organisations, with deliveries continuing through the second decade of the twenty first century.

Rafale B302, the second serial production Rafale B, configured with SCALP EG air launched cruise missile during trials. MBDA

DOMESTIC DELIVERIES – A 2008 White Paper had outlined the French Governments approval in principal for funding the acquisition of 300 Rafale aircraft for domestic customers (Dassault AR, 2008a). The following year, Dassault received notification of a contract for 60 Rafale, bringing total French domestic orders to 180 (Dassault AR, 2009), noted above. By 2013, it was clear that French requirements for Rafale numbers had been reduced to 225 (Dassault AR, 2013) – by the end of that year, 126 Rafale had been delivered to the domestic customer, including ten delivered in 2005 (Dassault AR, 2005); thirteen delivered in 2007 (Dassault AR, 2007); fourteen delivered in 2008 (Dassault AR, 2008); fourteen delivered in 2009 (Dassault AR, 2009); eleven delivered in 2010 (Dassault AR, 2010); eleven delivered in 2011 (Dassault AR, 2011); eleven delivered in 2012 (Dassault AR, 2012) and eleven delivered in 2013 (Dassault AR, 2013). The balance had been delivered in 2006 and prior to 2004. The last six of the eleven Rafale delivered in 2013 were the first of the 4th production series delivered to F3-04T Standard (Dassault AR, 2013). Eleven Rafale were delivered in 2014 (Dassault AR, 2014); five were delivered in 2015 (Dassault AR, 2015); six were delivered in 2016 (Dassault AR, 2016); one was delivered in 2017 (Dassault AR, 2017) and three were delivered in 2018 – by the end of 2018, the French domestic customer had received 152 of the 180 Rafale ordered (Dassault AR, 2018).

Trio of Egyptian Rafale B over Suez. Safran

EXPORT – Egypt had ordered 24 Rafale on 16 February 2015 (the first confirmed export contract for Rafale) (Dassault AR, 2014). To facilitate the delivery of three Rafale to Egypt that year – the three Rafale B were handed over to Egypt on 20 July 2015 – deliveries of French domestic customer Rafale were cut from eleven the previous year to five, and plans were initiated to increase production to three Rafale per month in 2018, to facilitate export delivery schedules (Dassault AR, 2015). A further three Rafale B were delivered to Egypt in 2016, followed by delivery of eight Rafale in 2017 (Dassault AR, 2017). A further nine Rafale were delivered to Egypt in 2018 (Dassault AR, 2018) and the last of the 24 ordered was delivered on 24 July 2019 (Dassault AR, 2019).

Qatar ordered 24 Rafale on 4 May 2015, with an option on twelve more (Dassault AR, 2015), which was converted on 7 December 2017, bringing the Qatar order to 36 with a new option placed on 36 more (Dassault AR, 2017). The first Rafale for Qatar was handed over on 6 February 2019 (Dassault AR, 2018).

India had indicated an intention to order Rafale in January 2012 (Dassault AR, 2012) and on 10 April 2015, India intimated her intention to finalise an order for 36 aircraft that year (Dassault AR, 2015) – in the event, this order was finalised on 23 September 2016 (Dassault AR, 2016) and the first Rafale for India, BI008, conducted its maiden flight on 30 October 2018 (Dassault AR, 2018). Under the offset agreements of the Indian contract, the DRAL (Dassault Reliance Aerospace Limited) joint venture was set up, from which the first components, Rafale engine bay doors, were delivered in 2019 (Dassault AR, 2019).

Deliveries of French Rafale, to fulfill the remaining 28 aircraft of the 180 ordered, were scheduled to resume in 2022. Although no new Rafale aircraft were delivered to the French domestic customer in 2019, two modernised aircraft were delivered to the French Navy (apparently to F3-R, but possibly to F3-04T Standard) (Dassault AR, 2019). With deliveries to the French domestic customer suspended until 2022, fulfilling the export orders became the main focus from 2018. To this end, 26 Rafale had been delivered to export customers in 2019 (Dassault AR, 2019). Planning was for 13 Rafale deliveries to export operators in 2020 (Dassault AR, 2019) – Greece having indicated her intention to order 18 Rafale on 12 September that year (Dassault PR, 2020) and the deliveries of several Rafale to India, in effect marking the entry to service of Rafale in that nation.

Previous page: The first Rafale for Qatar, QA202. This page: The first Rafale for India, BI008 (top). The Indian order covered two-seat and single seat Rafale (bottom) Dassault Aviation/Dassault Aviation-S. Randé/Dassault Aviation-C. Cosmao

3

RAFALE B/C/M

The Rafale concept, intended to replace all tactical combat aircraft in French domestic service, combined high agility, low-observability and high load carrying capability traits within a moderate size airframe. To accomplish intended mission roles it was intended from the outset of the program that Rafale would be designed as an omnirole platform equipped with new generation sensors and advanced weaponry. Rafale was designed to embrace the four operational traits of versatility, interoperability, flexibility and survivability within the omnirole concept, which called for the capability to conduct several operational functions simultaneously. An example of this capability would be the launch of air to air missile(s) against an airborne threat whilst the aircraft was conducting a penetration mission against a ground target at low altitude (Dassault, 2020). Although changing over several decades, the basic Rafale operational doctrine was the ability to fly omnirole missions with full interoperability with other assets of national or coalition origin. Thales summed up the operational requirement as follows:

> "Versatility to perform different missions; Interoperability to fight in coalition with the allies, synergy of the effects, in order to collectively produce the combination of effects better adapted to the tactical situation; Flexibility to conduct several different missions in the course of the same sortie; Reversibility to instantly switch from a coercion mission to a preventative mission or even to cancel a mission at the last second" and the "capability to last in a highly threatened environment", courtesy of the traits of low observable, often discrete sensors, and electronic warfare complex etc. (Thales, 2013).

A high degree of commonality was designed into the serial Rafale B/C/M in regard to airframe and systems/equipment, facilitated in no small measure by the fact that all three variants had comparable operational roles. This allowed the Rafale B/C/M to be built on a common airframe. The Rafale B incorporates a second cockpit section, absent in the Rafale C/M, whilst the Rafale M tricycle undercarriage (single main wheel units retracting into the fuselage and twin nose wheel unit retracting to lay in the forward fuselage underside) was optimised for the high sink rates associated with aircraft carrier landings, and incorporated structural enhancements to the airframe – an arrestor hook is accommodated in the rear fuselage under section. The airframe is stressed to take *g* forces of +9/-3.2. Maximum speed in afterburner was set at Mach 1.8 (would reduce in-line with stores weight values) with an operating ceiling up to at least 15240 m (Dassault, 2020).

Page 62: Single Seat Rafale C. Page 63: The Rafale design incorporates a standard tricycle undercarriage layout with single wheel main units and a twin wheel nose unit shown on Rafale B (top). The Rafale M adopted an undercarriage design optimised for the aircraft carrier operating environment, the most prominent change being the increased length nose unit oleo strut (bottom). Dassault Aviation/Safran-Jean-Francoise-Damios/Author

This page: French Air Force. Rafale B (foreground) configured with 2 x SCALP EG subsonic cruise missiles, wingtip mounted MICA air to air missiles and 3 x 2000 litre subsonic flight capable external fuel tanks and Rafale C (background) configured with 6 x MICA and 3 x 1250 litre supersonic flight capable external fuel tanks. Dassault Aviation/Dassault Aviation-K. Tokunaga

Basic dimensions of the serial Rafale include: length, 15.30 m; height, 5.30 m and wingspan, 10.90 m. Empty weight was put at just under 10000 kg (10 tonne) and maximum take-off weight was set at ~24493 kg (24.49 tonne). The efficiency of the 2 x M88-2 afterburning turbofan engines, each of which was rated at around 7.7 ton thrust, allowed Rafale to haul an external stores load of some 9072 kg (9.072 tonne) accommodated on 14 stores stations (13 on Rafale M). The five heavy load stores stations were designed wet (plumed for fuel transfer), allowing the carriage of up to five external fuel tanks (combined capacity of ~4672 kg (~4.67 tonne) leaving ~6667 kg (~6.67 tonne) for munitions or sensor pod carriage (Dassault, 2020).

When operating at maximum take-off weight – maximum fuel and stores loadout – Rafale could get airborne at about 2.5 times its empty weight, a capability not routinely emulated by any other aircraft in its weight class (Dassault, 2020).

BUDDY REFUELLING SYSTEM – A buddy refuelling pod capability was developed for Rafale operations in the absence of the availability of dedicated airborne refuelling assets (Dassault, 2020). By the early 2000's, the integration and trials for the Intertechnique buddy refuelling system for the naval Rafale had been completed. The first serial produced Rafale M, M1, was utilised to successfully refuel other Rafale and Dassault Super Etendard strike fighters to clear the system for operation from the F2 Standard Rafale M. The refueling pod was initially cleared for carriage at flight speeds up to Mach 0.9 indicated air speed. In-flight refueling had apparently been conducted at transfer rates in excess of 500 litres per minute in a speed/altitude range in the region of ~555 km/h (~300 knots) at altitudes of around 6100 m, with planned expansion to altitudes in excess of 9000 m (Harkins, 2004).

Rafale range could be extended through the carriage of external fuel tanks and in-flight refuelling. The Rafale M can also refuel other aircraft in flight. This Rafale M is configured with 2 x 2000 litre external fuel tanks carried on the inner wing stations, an inflight refuelling pod on centre fuselage stations and MICA IR air to air missiles on the wing intermediate and wingtip stations. Dassault Aviation- K. Tokunaga

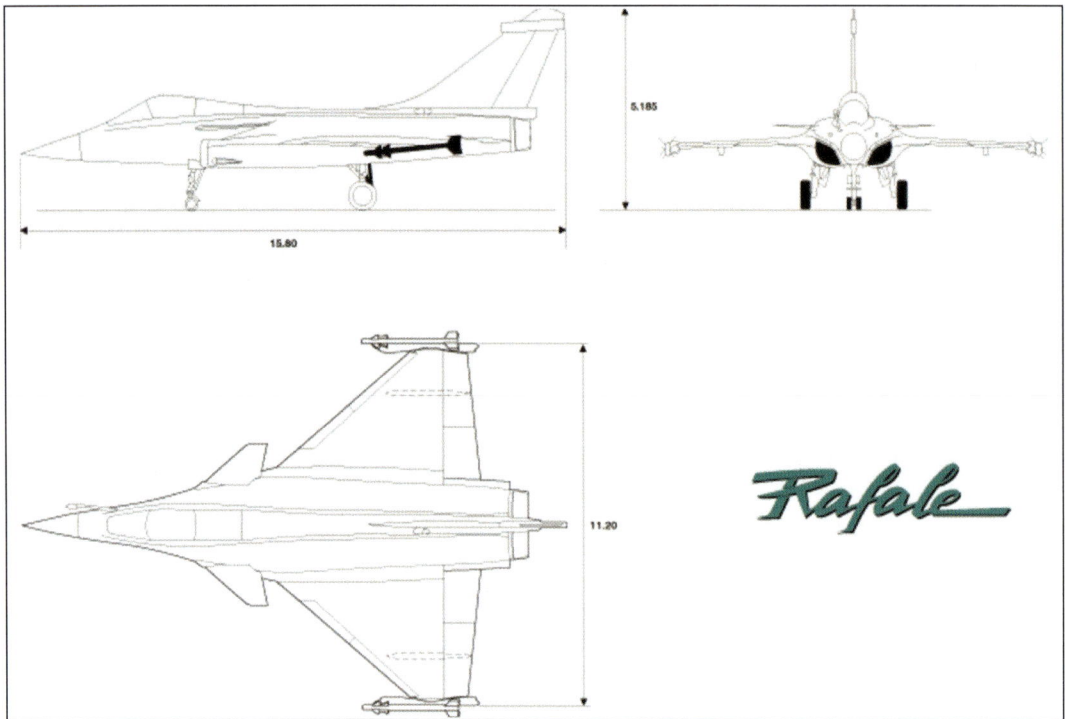

Single-seat Rafale general arrangement 3-view. Dimensions: Length, 15.80 m; height, 5.185 m and wingspan, 11.20 m, indicate that it is representative of the Rafale A01 demonstrator Dassault Aviation

LOW OBSERVABLE – In line with designing an aircraft that would be discrete in its operation in order to reduce vulnerability to countermeasures, attention was paid toward arriving at a low radar cross section value, within constraints of cost and mission. This was accomplished through a combination of the Rafale design relatively small dimensions, outer lines and manufacture materials. While some of the low-observable enhancement measures adopted remain classified as of 2020, it is possible to outline certain design traits contributing to the Rafale low radar cross section, such as serrated features on the wing and canard trailing edges (Dassault, 2020).

The airframe was designed for several decades of service, the Mirage 2000 generation gauge free concept being employed to monitor fatigue levels. The airframe is manufactured predominantly from composite materials (these materials make up 70% of the Rafale 'wetted' area), which contributes to the design excellent maximum take-off to empty weight value – this is put at around 40% that of legacy aircraft designs of predominantly aluminium/titanium construction (Dassault, 2020).

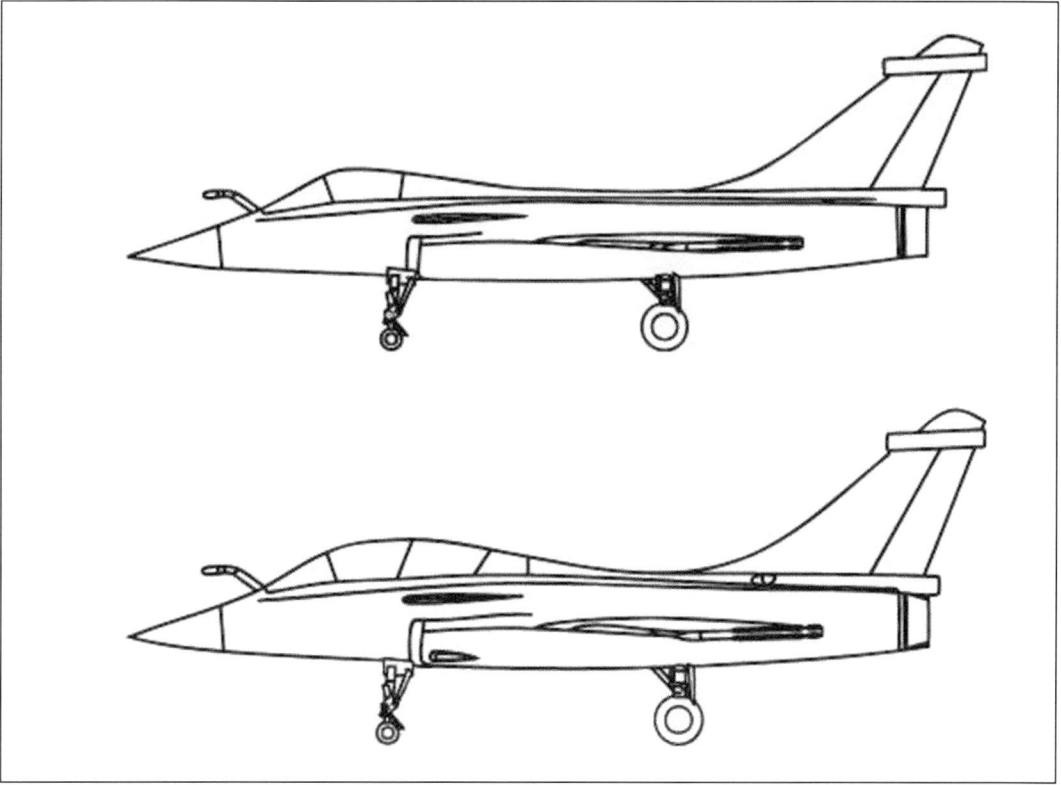

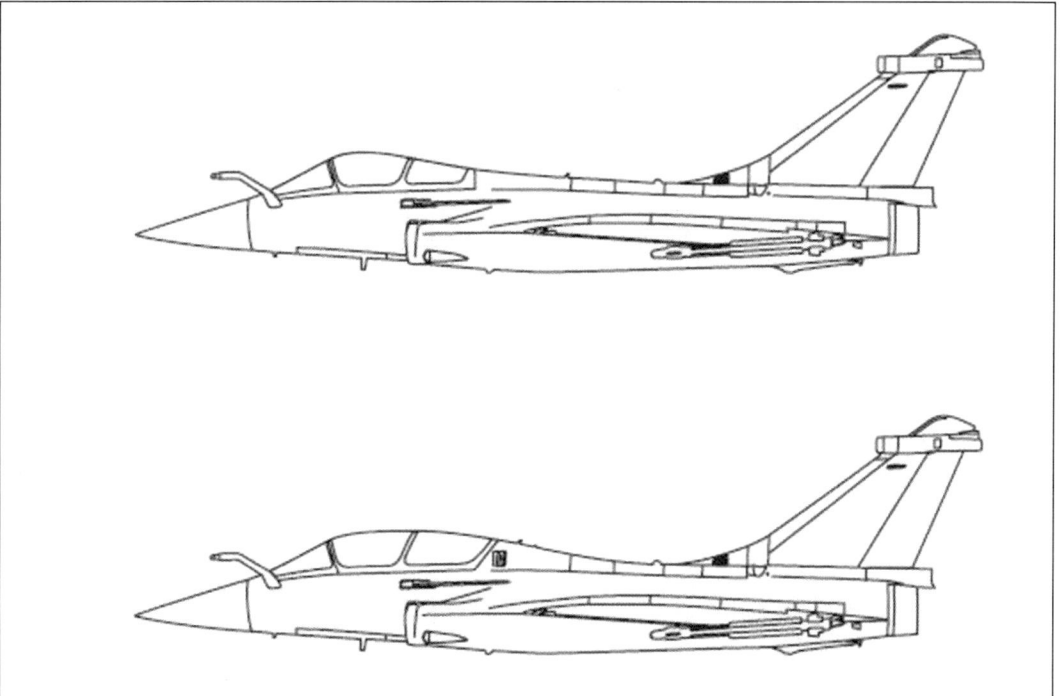

Rafale C (upper) and Rafale B (lower) profile drawings with undercarriage deployed (top) and retracted (bottom). Dassault Aviation

Port side profile drawings of Rafale B (top), Rafale C (centre) and Rafale M (bottom). Dassault Aviation-F. Fischer

Among the low observable features of the Rafale design are serrated features on the wing and canard trailing edges, shown to advantage on a Rafale C. Dassault Aviation-K. Tokunaga

CLOSE-COUPLED CANARD/DELTA WING – The canard-delta Rafale can be defined as a direct descendant of the long line of Mirage fighters, which had culminated with the Mirage 2000/4000, initially developed concurrently. Embracing design technology advances, Rafale introduced a forward canard, close-coupled with the delta wing. This decision was taken on the strength of computational fluid dynamics data that demonstrated the benefits of the close-coupled canard/wing arrangement. Overall test data indicated that the close-coupled canard/wing arrangement provisioned for a more comprehensive range of centre-of-gravity locations to suit the full-spectrum of flight conditions, facilitating smooth handling of the aircraft throughout the entire flight envelope. The close coupled canard/wing configuration contributed significantly to the exemplary performance of Rafale, such as the high range/payload performance for an aircraft in its weight class, maintaining high agility even when operating at high angles of attack (Dassault, 2020).

Previous page: The all-moving close-coupled canard/wing configuration shown on Rafale M01 at the Paris Air Salon in 1997. This page: The close-coupled canard/wing configuration facilitated excellent flight characteristics in all flight regimes. Author/Dassault Aviation

FLIGHT CONTROL SYSTEM – Rafale is equipped with a quadruple redundant FBW (Fly By Wire) FCS (Flight Control System), overseeing the function processes of aircraft handling and longitudinal stability. The quadruple redundancy is provided through three digital and a single analogue channel with no recourse to mechanical backup. Autonomy between channels is built into the system in order to avoid the potential for an anomaly in one channel being present in the remaining three channels (Dassault, 2020).

The FCS provides for efficient flight in all cleared load out configurations and all flight regimes, in environmental conditions of fair or adverse weather. For operations at low altitude the FCS operates in terrain following mode (Dassault, 2020), a trait that would increase the aircraft survivability in the event it was called on to operate in airspace protected by advanced air defence systems, such as that offered by the Russian S-400/Pantsir combination.

SAFRAN'S CONTRIBUTION TO THE
RAFALE
(DASSAULT AVIATION)

—

M88 ENGINES

AUXILIARY POWER UNIT (APU)

INERTIAL NAVIGATION SYSTEM

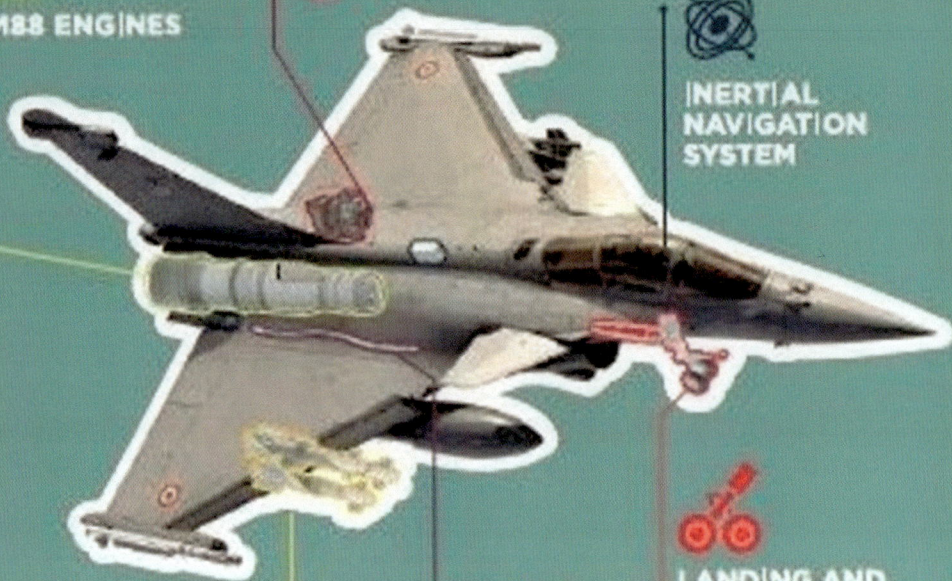

LANDING AND BRAKING SYSTEMS

WIRING

AASM MODULAR PRECISION GUIDED WEAPON

OTHER SYSTEMS AND EQUIPMENT

POWER TRANSMISSION SYSTEM

ENGINE CONTROL UNIT

FILTERS (hydraulic, air, oil)

EJECTION SEATS

SAFRAN

Previous page: Infographic illustrating the contribution to the Rafale program made by Safran. This page: Full-scale model of the Safran (previously SNECMA) M88-2 engine developed for the Rafale. Dassault Aviation/Author

ENGINE – As briefly recounted in the previous chapter the serial produced Rafale was to be powered by two SNECMA (later Safran) M88-2 afterburning turbofan engines. The two major factors influencing the decision to adopt a twin-engine configuration for Rafale was the increased power availability and flight safety inherent in twin engine aircraft that is not present in a single engine design. The standard of main power plant installed in the initial F1 Standard Rafale was the M88-2, each of which was rated at ~50 kN (~5098 kgf) dry thrust and ~75 kN (~7648 kgf) when variable-area afterburner was employed (Harkins, 2004 & Dassault Aviation).

In 1970, SNECMA had commenced design studies into technologies for future combat aircraft power plants beyond the M53 studies intended for what would emerge as the Mirage 2000/4000 series tactical combat aircraft. A number of research establishments were brought into the studies in cooperation with SNECMA. The program that would eventually produce the M88 was formally launched in 1977, as technology advancements increased the potential to arrive at an engine significantly more advanced than the Atar series powering Mirage III/5/50/F1 series combat aircraft and the SNECMA M53, then in development for the Mirage 2000/4000 (Harkins, 2004).

Rafale M01 engages afterburner on the installed M88-2 turbofan engines at the commencement of its take-off run at Farnborough in September 1996. Author

The non-flight rated SNECMA M88-1 commenced a 200-hour bench run series in January 1984 (the full development was launched in 1986). A program of bench tests for the flight-rated M88-2, (formerly M88-1.5) commenced on 27 February 1989. No less than nine M88-2 were allocated to terrestrial test functions, although the last was apparently modified to flight standard and installed in the port engine bay of Rafale A01, the aircraft retaining a General Electric F404-GE-400 turbofan engine in the starboard engine bay. As recounted in chapter 1, Rafale A01 flew in this asymmetric engine configuration on 27 February 1990. Seven test flights were conducted with the M88-2 engine in Rafale A01 before it was replaced with a flight rated M88-2 engine from a pre-production (development) batch of fifteen intended to power the Rafale development (prototypes). The M88 received certification on 30 October 1992, full qualification was received in April 1996 and serial deliveries commenced on 30 December that year – some 4,424 hours of flight testing in around 12,666 hours had been accomplished on the Rafale development aircraft by that date (this value would include ground based engine testing) (Harkins, 2004).

The sole Rafale C prototype, C01, undergoing a starboard M88-2 engine change. Safran

The M88 basic characteristics include overall length, ~3.537 cm (139.29 in) and weight, ~897 kg (~1,977.55 lb.). The Rafale inlet diameter measured ~0.695 m (27.40 in). The M88 was designed as a lightweight, twin-shaft augmented turbofan featuring a three stage fan, six stage HP (High Pressure) compressor discs of composite material, one HP turbine, one LP (Low Pressure) turbine, a by-pass ratio of 0.3 and a pressure ratio of 24.5. The engine featured a Safran (previously SNECMA) developed FADEC (Full Authority Digital Engine Control) system with built in redundancy, which increased engine reliability, safety and mission effectiveness through handling minor engine faults without the need to inform the crew (Harkins, 2004). FADEC provisions for carefree handling over the full flight envelope – the engine can apparently be throttled from idle to full afterburner sub-three seconds.

Ease of maintenance was enhanced over previous generation engines – the M88-2 incorporated twenty one interchangeable modules, which were equipped with line replaceable units. A complete engine change can be accomplished in the region of one hour under base maintenance conditions. The M88 is accessed through a series of panels on the undersides of the respective engine bays, the engine being lowered down when removal is required (Dassault, 2020 & Harkins, 2004).

Top: Exhaust nozzle of M88-2 engines on the Rafale assembly line. Bottom: Rafale M1 engages afterburner on installed M88-2 turbofans during flight testing at Istres (13) on 13 June 2006. Dassault Aviation

The M88 engine design concept called for high thrust to weight ratio, reliability, ease of maintenance and low operating costs. To achieve this the M88 was developed in a stepped approach, employing advanced technologies and materials in construction, including incorporation of composite materials and ceramic coatings. The first twenty nine serial produced M88-2 engines were delivered to Step 1 standard. All subsequent M88-2 would be delivered to Step 4 standard. The changes incorporated in the M88-2 Step 4 included introducing three-dimensional HP compressor and turbine blades (blisks) – one piece integral blades in the compressor disks – advanced cooling channels for the combustion chamber, improved thermal coatings on the HP turbine blades (single crystal) and an extended time between overhaul without any notable loss in power output (Dassault, 2020 & Harkins, 2004).

An M88-2 improvement program, referred to as TCO (Total Cost of Ownership), was launched in 2008. This was primarily aimed at reducing costs through improving engine operation endurance. Safran engines enhanced the high-pressure compressor and high pressure turbine through introduction of increased strength components and improved cooling, increasing durability by around 50%. Maintenance requirements were reduced through enhancements to extend service life of some engine modules. Further development of the M88 by Safran led to the M88-4E, which built on the M88-2 TCO program and introduced further improvements. Initial planning called for the M88-4E to be delivered in new production Rafale aircraft from 2012 (F3-04T and later F3-R Standard) (Dassault, 2020 & Safran Aircraft Engines, 2020).

The current (2020) service standard of M88 has a growth potential of 20%. Work to further update the M88 had commenced at Safran in January 2019. This work was two-pronged – for updating then current service Rafale Standards and to power the Rafale F4 Standard, estimated to debut in 2024 (2020 planning estimate). In regard to the M88 engine, Standard 4 focusses on electronic enhancements on the engine itself and on the Rafale aircraft overall (specifically in the electronic engine control) as well as ground based elements. The enhancements are intended to provision for faster data transfer and greater data storage from the aircraft to ground stations for analysis, with the aim of improving maintenance predictions (Safran Aircraft Engines, 2020). Time required for removal and reinstallation of one engine is one hour for two ground technicians (Dassault Aviation).

M88 characteristics/performance – data furnished by Safran Aircraft Engines

Length: ~3.537 cm (139.29 in)
Inlet diameter: ~0.695 m (27.40 in)
Weight: ~897 kg (~1,977.55 lb.)
Thrust, dry: ~5098 kgf (11,240 lbf.) (Dassault data puts M88-2 dry thrust at a value of ~4791 kgf (10,971 lbf.) – the value differences may depend on engine standards
Thrust, afterburner: ~7648 kgf (16,860 lbf.) (Conflicting Safran documentation states ~7484 kgf (16,500 lbf.) and Dassault data states ~7538 kgf (16,620 lbf.) – the value differences may depend on standards
Specific fuel consumption, dry power: ~0.35 kg/kgf/h (0.78 lb./lbf./h)
Specific fuel consumption with afterburner: ~0.75 kg/kgf/h (1.66 lb./lbf./h)
Airflow rate: ~65 kg/s (143.30 lb./s)
Turbine temperature: Entry, 1,850 Kelvin (~1,576.85° C (Celsius)/~2,870.6° F (Fahrenheit), inlet ~1,773.15 Kelvin (1,500° C/~2732° F
Pressure ratio: 24.50
Bypass ratio: 0.30
Time required to reach maximum power: 4 seconds

Previous page: Rafale M1 at Istres (13) on 13 June 2006, showing to effect the external layout of the engine air intakes. This page bottom: The Rafale crew is accommodated on MkF16F zero-zero ejection-seat(s) located beneath a cockpit canopy that hinges to starboard, easing complexity of seat removal/maintenance. This page top: Rafale M02 on the Istres runway during the M88-4E (Pack CGP) test campaign. Safran-Eric Drouin/Safran/Safran-Eric Drouin

Martin Baker was a partner in the Rafale program from its earliest days. As the program progressed, SEMMB (a consortium of Safran and Martin Baker France) was formed to develop and produce the MkF16F zero-zero ejection-seat common to all serial Rafale variants – B/C/M. The image above depicts a demonstration model of the MkF16F on a Rafale forward fuselage mock-up. Author

EJECTION SEAT – The cockpit canopy on the Rafale M hinges to starboard and features a frameless windscreen forward section. In the event of an emergency requiring evacuation from the aircraft, the MkF16F zero-zero ejection-seat, developed by SEMMB (a consortium of Safran and Martin Baker France), propels the occupant(s) away from the aircraft at a velocity of 15 m/s. The seat, which weighs 90 kg, can be broken down to a number of constituent parts, among which are the head & parachute unit, harness, ejection handle, seat pan with adjustable height settings and the survival pack – this contains an emergency beacon, life raft, medical first aid kit, water and food (Safran, 2020).

The ejection sequence, which from start to parachute deployment, lasts some 2 seconds, is as follows: 0.00 second, activation of the ejection handle initiates canopy shattering for seat and occupant ejection from the aircraft; 0.20 second, the rocket powered phase propels the seat from the aircraft at acceleration forces from 14-22 *g*; 0.30 second, the seat commences deceleration at the end of the rocket powered phase; 0.40 second, the drogue parachute deploys; 1.00 second, main parachute canopy is extracted; 1.35 seconds, the pilot is separated from the seat as the main parachute canopy deploys; 2.00 seconds, the main parachute canopy is fully open and the survival pack is extended on a line as the pilot descends to the surface (Safran, 2020).

Good all-round view is afforded by the high placing of the seat, which affords the pilot enhanced *g*-protection due to its 29° inclination (Dassault), a modest reduction from the 32° inclination on the Rafale A demonstrator.

The cockpit is furnished with an air conditioning system, contributing to the comfortable environment afforded the crew (Dassault, 2020). The main avionics equipment bay is located behind the pilot, with two more lateral equipment bays port and starboard of the cockpit.

All variants of the Rafale, B/C/M (F2 Standard Rafale M2 illustrated), are equipped with the SEMMB MkF16F zero-zero ejection-seat. USN

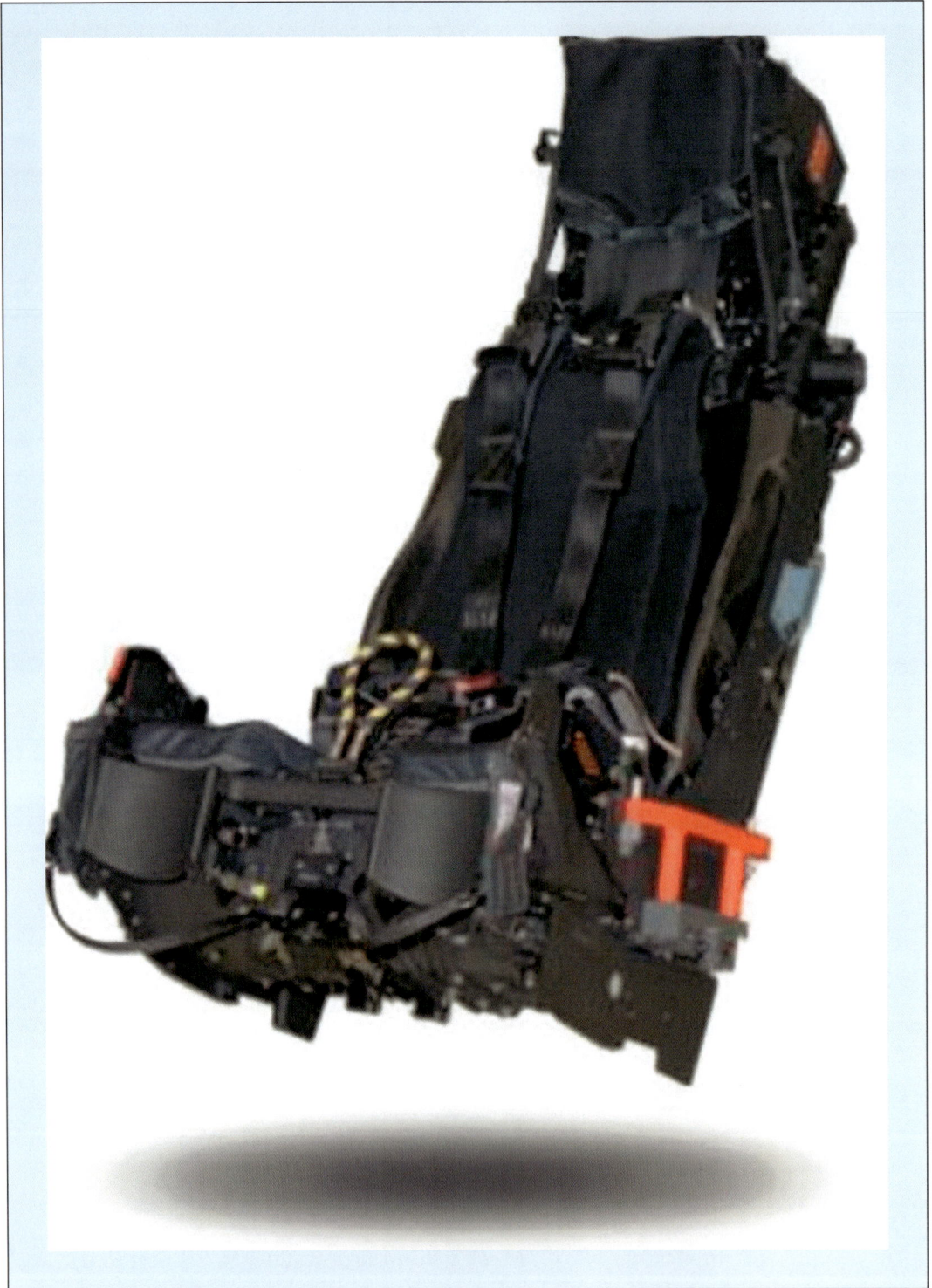

SEMMB MkF16F zero-zero ejection-seat. Safran

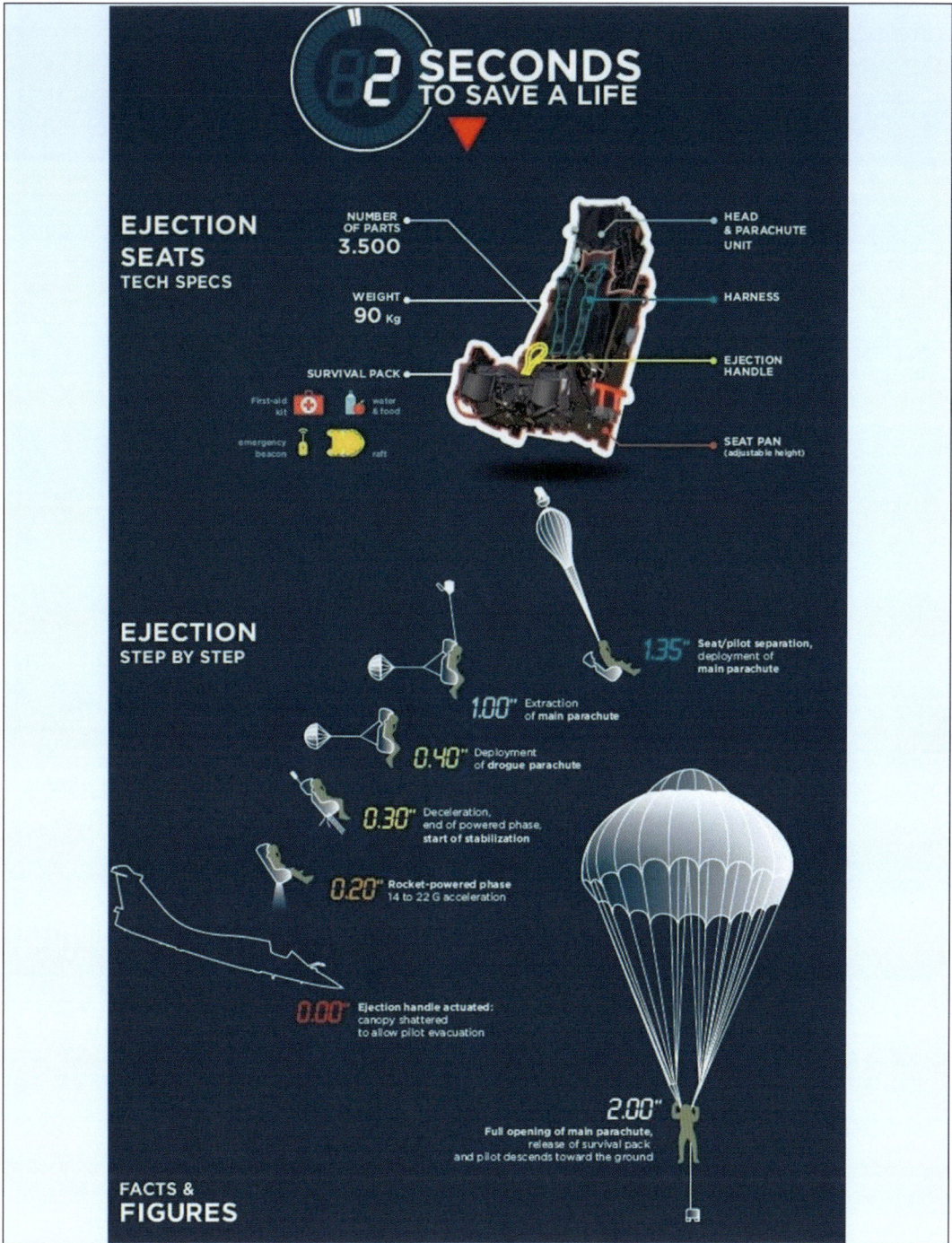

Graphic detailing the constituent parts and ejection sequence of the SEMMB MkF16F zero-zero ejection-seat. Safran

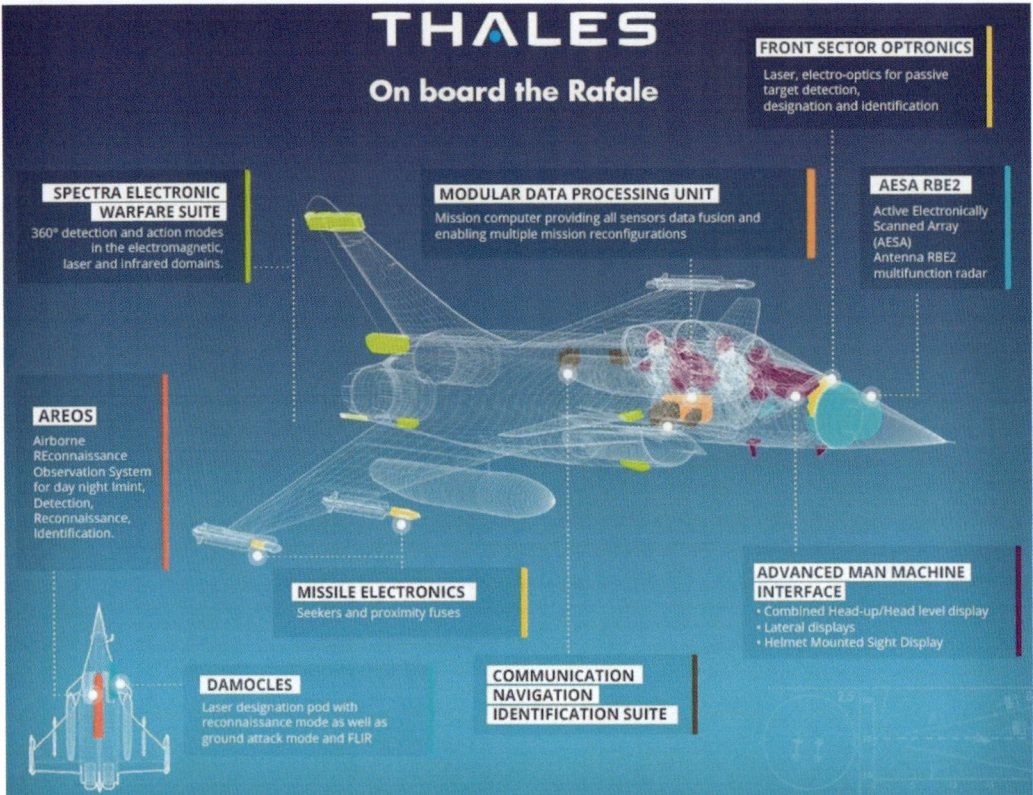

Infographic illustrating the contribution of Thales to the Rafale program – SPECTRA, Modular Data Processing Unit, AESA RBE2, AREOS, DAMOCLES, Missile electronics, Communication Navigation Identification suite and Advanced Man Machine Interface. Dassault Aviation

MAN MACHINE INTERFACE – At the heart of the MMI (Man [human] Machine Interface) is the HOTAS (Hands-On Throttle and Stick), multifunction display screens along with the other major components – combined HUD (Heads-Up Display)/HL (Head-Level) display. The overall MMI provides the pilot with a wide-filed of view in frontal, rear and lateral aspects (Dassault, 2020).

The 30° x 22° wide-angle heliographic HUD reproduces mission data pertaining to aircraft flight parameters and immediate tactical information for short term (or immediate) mission tasking(s). Mission system data is displayed and managed on the two laterally mounted touch screen cockpit displays. The 20° x 20° HL display correlates data from available sensor systems into a large format easy to read colour-coded picture (requires no significant interpretation skills, allowing quick understanding and decision making). The HL display, data from which is presented to the pilot at the same optical distance as data presented on the HUD to facilitate ease of transition between viewing both displays, is employed in medium to long term mission tasking(s) (Dassault, 2020). The lateral colour touch display screens (port and starboard) are utilised for management of data from various systems (Dassault, 2020 & Thales). The MMI can be enhanced through the addition of a pilot Helmet Mounted Sight Display (Thales).

The Rafale cockpit is dominated by the advanced man machine interface between crew and sensors, at the heart of which is the HUD, with HL display below, and two lateral multifunction display screens. Dassault Aviation-Alex Paringaux

FUSED SENSORS – Data garnered by Rafale advanced sensors – AESA (Active Electronically Scanned Array) RBE2, FSO (Front Sector Optronics), SPECTRA (*Systéme de Protection et d'Evitement des Conduites de Tire dee Rafale* /Self-Protection Equipment to Counter Threats for Rafale Aircraft) EW (Electronic Warfare), IFF (Identification Friend or Foe), infrared seekers incorporated in MICA IR missile and the aircraft data-link (Link 16 or national compliant) – is fused in a process referred to as multi-sensor data-fusion. This presents operators with an enhanced tactical picture, increasing overall situational awareness. (Dassault, 2020).

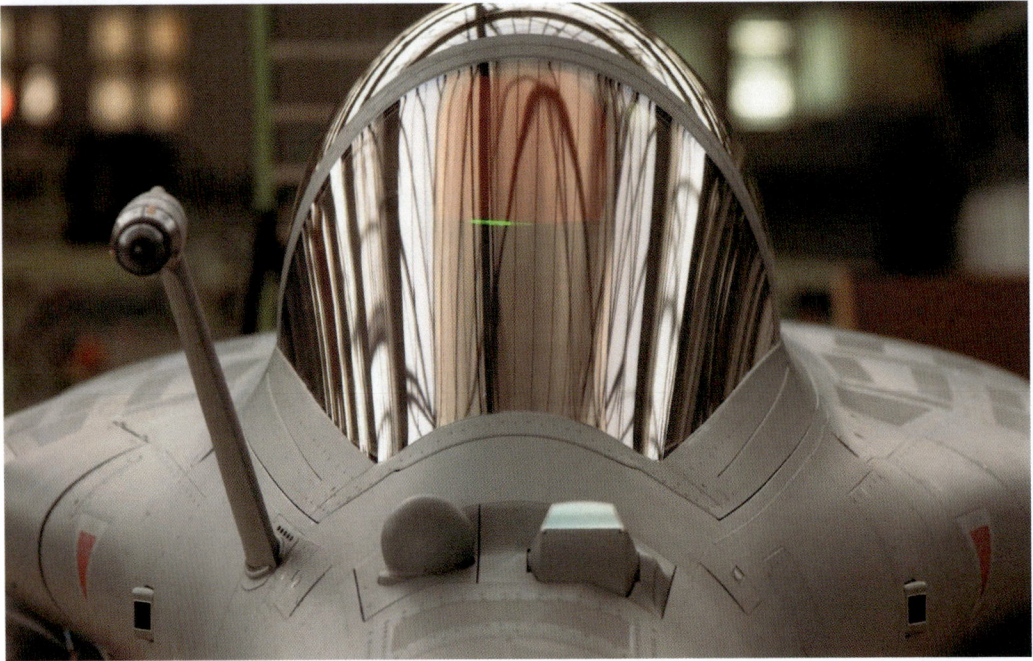

For close-range and flight parameter data presentation, Rafale is endowed with a 30° x 22° wide-angle heliographic HUD positioned behind the frameless windscreen. Dassault Aviation

MDPU – At the heart of the Rafale advanced sensor capabilities is the MDPU (Modular Data Processing Unit), which incorporates COTS (Commercial (Common) Off The Shelf) technologies. The MDPU is the main mission computer facilitating the fusion of data from on-board sensors – radar, FSO, SPECTRA EW, IFF interrogator, data-link and podded systems, such as AREOS, DAMOCLES and MICA IR seeker head. The MDPU comprises nineteen LRU (Line Replaceable Units), any one of which provides processing power in the order of 50 times that incorporated in a legacy aircraft design, such as the Mirage 2000 (Dassault, 2020).

The multi-sensor data fusion concept calls for correlation of mission data from a number of systems to produce a simplified overall tactical picture on the cockpit tactical display screens. This reduces pilot workload and enhances the ability to arrive at an informed decision through increased situational awareness. The three-stage process of automated data fusion provides a number of advantages over individual sensor picture(s) as it overcomes some individual sensor limitations in regard to certain areas, such as wavelength etc. (Dassault, 2020).

The MDPU is at the heart of the ability to integrate a diversity of weapon systems on the Rafale platform – Rafale B (foreground) is configured with SCALP EG air to surface cruise missiles and MICA IR air to air missiles, whilst Rafale C (background) is configured with MICA EM and MICA IR. Dassault Aviation

The MDPU was central to the overall increase in capability of the various Rafale Standards, facilitating integration of new systems and weapons – the MIL-STD-1760 compliant stores management system provisions for integration of new weapon systems (Dassault, 2020). The MDPU was designed to be adapted as new processing technology became available, allowing the system to remain relevant in an age of ever accelerating digital/data technology advances (Dassault, 2020).

COMMUNICATION NAVIGATION IDENTIFICATION SUITE – The Communication Navigation Identification suite was developed as a system to oversee the operation of a number of on-board systems, notably the, ECCM (Electronic Counter Counter Measures), IFF and data-link (Thales).

DATA-LINK – The integral Link-16 (NATO (North Atlantic Treaty Organisation) compliant secure high speed data-link allowed information to be shared with and received from other airborne platforms and surface based elements of the command and control infrastructure, thereby increasing overall tactical situational awareness of all linked data-sharer/receivers. This capability, combined with the data-fusion concept, transforms aircraft in the class of Rafale into battle management platforms rather than individual strike/defensive platforms (Dassault, 2020). Potential operators not cleared for Link-16 operation can integrate other data-link standards to meet their specific requirements (Dassault, 2020).

NET-CENTRIC – The open architecture concept, data fusion software and data-link system, afford the Rafale its net-centric capability through coalescing the platform into the overall integrated tactical operation space able to exchange data. The ROVER (Remotely Operated Video Enhanced Receiver) is central to the net-centrality of Rafale, facilitating the transfer of and sharing of images and videos with other assets, such as ground stations (Dassault, 2020).

Rafale C137 was the first Rafale to be equipped with the AESA RBE2, circa 2013 (illustrated is Rafale B320 equipped with the AESA). Thales-Eric Raz

As noted in the above sections, the Rafale main mission systems, such as the RBE2 radar, FSO and SPECTRA are closely integrated with data from all systems fused into a single tactical image, providing the pilot a clear easy to read picture of the tactical situation, significantly enhancing situational awareness.

RADAR – The primary sensor for Rafale was to be an advanced radar complex that emerged as the multifunctional ESA (Electronically Scanned Array) (later the AESA was introduced) RBE2 (*Radar a Balayage Electronic 2 plans*/two axis electronic scanning radar) developed by Thales. The AESA RBE2 was designed and developed for short and long range operation and the ability to track multiple air to air or air to surface targets, whilst continuing to scan for other potential threats/targets (Thales, 2013b).

The phased array is a major leap in technology compared with conventional mechanical scanning radar. Advances include increased efficiency, increased reliability and increased protection against detection for the host platform through negation of the requirement to point the antenna at the target (Thales & Harkins, 2004).

When the Rafale program was authorised in the 1980's, it had been considered that the Thomson-CSF RDX radar complex would be installed in the serial design. Thomson-CSF had a wealth of experience in designing radar systems for combat aircraft, producing the RDI complex for the Mirage 2000C and later the RDY for the Mirage 2000-5/9 respectively (the RBE2 development was underway simultaneously with that of the RDY). The RDX, referred to as the RACAAS (*Radar de Combat Aéiren et d'Ataque au Sol*), was flown for the first time in a CEV (*Centre d'Essais en Vol*) operated Dassault Mystere 20 test-bed in late 1986. This system was plagued by development problems. In 1987, Electronique Serge Dassault (later Dassault Electronique) joined the ACE (*Avion de Combat European*) consortium, formed in April 1987, and forwarded the proposal of an improved development of the Antelope 5 radar (then under development for the Mirage 2000N nuclear strike aircraft and Mirage 2000D ground-attack aircraft) as an alternative to the troubled RDX (RDXE2). The Antelope derivative became known as the Antelope 50. Flight trials of this radar commenced aboard a CEV Dassault Mystere 20 test-bed in 1988. On 1 December that year, the French Defence Minister ordered both teams to combine their respective efforts for the RDX and Antelope 50 into a single program under the auspices of GIE (*Groupment Interet Economique*), for which Thomson-CSF had design leadership. A formal development contract for the new radar, then known as the RBG (*Radar du Bord du GIE*), was placed by the DGA (*Délégué Général pour l'armament*/General Delegate for Armament) on 13 April 1989. The contract stipulated commencement of flight testing in 1991, which would prove to be over ambitious. A full-scale development contract was awarded on 29 November 1990, by which time the radar designation had changed to RBE2. The details of the contract included construction of twelve development radar sets – the initial three were to be incorporated into a ground development/test program with the balance allocated to airborne trials aboard flying laboratories and up to three of the planned Rafale development aircraft (Harkins, 2004). Flight tests of a Falcon 20 flying laboratory (former RDI radar test-bed), equipped with a functional ESA RBE2 radar system, commenced at Brétigny-sur-Orge, near Paris, on 10 July 1992. A further Falcon 20 laboratory and a Mirage 2000 were flown with functional RBE2 radar installed, and the Rafale/RBE2 combination commenced flight test on 7 July 1993. Initial flight testing was conducted with development radar sets, serial produced units not being delivered until 1997 (Harkins, 2004).

Dassault Mirage 2000B laboratory equipped with an RBE2 development set for trials. Thales

Compact nose radar housing (top) and ESA RBE2 installed in Rafale B02 (bottom). Author/Thales

ESA/AESA RBE2 radar complex. Thales

The baseline air to air capability provisioned with the ESA RBE2 included the ability to track several tens of airborne targets simultaneously, eight of which could be engaged concurrently whilst the radar continued tracking the remaining targets. The air to surface capability (not available in the release cleared for F1 Standard) called for the ability to track several tens of targets simultaneously (Harkins, 2004).

Advantages of the ESA over mechanical scanning antenna includes the ability to track the full range of targets whilst searching for other targets at the optimum data garnering rate – this relates to targets not only inside the search volume, but also outside the search volume whilst mechanical scanning tracks only inside the search volume (Dassault, 2020). Mechanically scanned antenna are limited in capability as the steering mechanics generally move only a single antenna. For an antenna to be considered active, the forward part – made up of multiple (often several hundred) T/R (Transmit/Receive) modules amplifies radiated power and pre-amplifies received power. Among the advantages of an active antenna is that it speeds up the reaction time inordinately, but also provisions for the detection and tracking of multiple targets in a multitude of directions simultaneously. This is possible due to the fact that whilst the mechanically scanned antenna points the radiation beam in a single direction at speeds constrained by the mechanics of the assembly, in the active antenna, each individual T/R module can be directed at a target at electronics speeds in a process often referred to as 'electronic scanning in space' (Thales, 2013a). Adopting the active antenna also reduced weight and, potentially, the area of the overall radar complex through such measures as the active antenna not requiring the heavy mechanical steering mechanism. The active antenna also allowed for forgoing a radar transmitter and first stage of signal processing associated with mechanically steered antenna systems.

Beyond the initial service capability releases for the ESA/AESA RBE2, further updates were planned in line with introducing successive Rafale Standards – F2, F3 and F4 – to service, along with planning for Rafale export Standards. To this end, in April 2002, the DGA awarded Thales a contract covering development of an active array antenna demonstrator for the RBE2. This was flown on a Dassault Mystere test-bed operating from Cazaux in December 2002, before being flown in a Rafale in April 2003. Thales had apparently commenced initial design studies into technologies applicable to development of an active array antenna as far back as 1990 and such a system had initially been specified for the baseline export Rafale Standard in 1999 (Harkins, 2004).

C137, an F3 Standard Rafale C, was the first aircraft to be equipped with the AESA RBE2 on the assembly line. Dassault Aviation

It is unclear what downgrade changes, if any, have been made to the AESA RBE2 Standard equipping export standard Rafale – Rafale C depicted in Qatari livery. Dassault Aviation-M. Alleaume

The AESA replaced the ESA on the RBE2 with the introduction of Tranche 4 serial Rafale deliveries, circa 2012 (Dassault, 2020). The AESA RBE2, like the ESA, was developed as a multi-functional radar complex optimised for long-range detection, VMTWS (Versatile Multi-target Track While Scan), air to air and air to surface capability (Thales). With the introduction of the AESA – the first combat aircraft AESA to enter serial production in Europe – the baseline capability of the RBE2, in 2013, was at, or close to, the full capability standard specified. The radar was able to operate in several different modes simultaneously, providing a large diversity of functions: detect, track and oversee engagement of multiple targets in all-aspect look-up/look-down modes whilst operating day or night in adverse or fair weather conditions in an active electronic jamming environment; generation of three-dimensional surface maps in real-time to facilitate terrain following; generation of high resolution surface maps in real-time to aid navigation and targeting and operate in maritime mode for the detection and tracking of multiple sea surface targets (Thales, 2013a).

The extended range capability enhanced the RBE2 ability to detect low-observable targets, and the long-range detection capability, enhanced the potential for employment of the Meteor extended range beyond-visual range active radar guided air to air missile (Thales, 2013a), which was designed to engage airborne targets at ranges considerably beyond that attainable with the MICA EM active radar guided air to air missile.

Technical features of the AESA Antenna Block included: active electronic scanning; high reliability of the T/R modules and 'very low-side and scattered lobes' in both azimuth and elevation (Thales, 2013a). Technical features of the Active-transmit/receiver modules and exciter/receiver included: 'Multiple Waveforms; Coherent X Band frequency generation; Excellent spectral purity; Wide bandwidth; Full monopulse' and 'MMIC/GaAs technologies' (Thales, 2013a). Technical features of the programmable signal processor and data processor included: 'Target detection and ECCM processing; fully programmable; anti-obsolescence solutions; open architecture – COTS components; Tracking computation' and production of high-resolution map(s) (Thales, 2013a).

Rafale B320 equipped with the AESA RBE2. Dassault Aviation-Eric Raz

Capable of all-aspect look-down and look-up function, the AESA provisioned for detection and track of multiple airborne targets when operating on long-range interception down to close range air combat missions scenarios – targets would be automatically sorted and ranked in order of priority. The radar was designed to function in an electronic warfare active environment in natural environmental conditions of fair or adverse weather, day or night, in which MICA EM and Meteor radar guided air to air missiles were employed (Dassault, 2020 & Thales, 2013a).

The radar possesses a deep low-level airspace penetration capability with fully automatic terrain following and obstacle avoidance mode. Three-dimensional maps can be generated in real-time to aid terrain-following for low altitude penetration missions. High-resolution 2D (Dimensional) surface maps can be generated to provide navigational updates and to aid in identification and designation of surface targets. For strike operations the radar updates the target area data whilst the aircraft is en route and features a SAR (Synthetic Aperture Radar) high resolution imagery mode with high waveform agility. The AESA also built on the previous generation system to detect and track multiple maritime surface targets designated for engagement by cruise missiles flying several metres above the sea surface (Dassault, 2020 & Thales, 2013a). The AESA facilitates the radar ability to rapidly switch from one mode to another, allowing multiple functions to be conducted simultaneously – all operating modes feature high resistance to active jamming (Thales, 2013a).

Rafale M01 (previous page) deficient the FSO (OSF) complex present on the upper forward fuselage ahead of the cockpit windscreen on Rafale M02 (this page). Author

FSO (OSF) – Rafale is equipped with the FSO – Front Sector Optronics/OSF *Optronique Secteur Frontal* – complex, which is a laser/electro-optical suite optimised for passive (radar silent) target detection, identification and designation. Among the main features of the FSO is the ability to conduct passive detection of airborne threats day or night through a suite of high-resolution electro-optical and infrared spectrum sensors with a stated low false alarm rate. The system bestows upon the operator enhanced situational awareness, operating against air to air and air to surface threats (Thales, 2013b).

In the spring of 1991, a contract was placed with Thomson-CSF (now Thales) and SAT to produce the FSO and flight testing in a Dassault Mystere 20 laboratory commenced in April 1999. The system was later installed in Rafale M02 and B01 development aircraft and the first serial Rafale, B301, and later B302, for flight-testing and integration. In early 2001, Thales was contracted by the DGA for production of an initial batch of FSO – integration of the FSO with the ESA RBE2 had commenced the previous year to pave the way for introduction on the F2 Standard Rafale from 2004 (Harkins, 2004).

FSO infrared sensor ball, starboard, and television/laser module, port, for Rafale (top) and sensor images of air and surface targets (bottom). Thales

Rafale B powers up for take-off at Le Bourget in 2007. Safran- Jean-Christophe Moreau

A major advantage of the FSO over radar is its immunity to detection and radio-electronic jamming as it operates in the optical wavelengths (Dassault, 2020). Specific mission functions include tracking of airborne and surface targets day or night; IRST (InfraRed Search & Track); detection of targets at long-range in a wide 'Field Of Regard'; automatic search for and tracking of targets (in 3D); identification and range calculation of air to air and air to surface targets; increased overall host platform situational awareness and increased effectiveness of the overall weapon system (Thales). The identification channel featured the following functions: detection and tracking of targets; reconnaissance and object/area identification; laser range finding (eye safe) and generation of TV (Television) imagery (Thales, 2013b). The TV imaging allows targets to be observed, visually identified and tracked. The tele-lens captures a view of airborne or ground based targets, the range to which would be measured by the integral laser (Dassault, 2020).

The FSO, as with comparable systems in service on Eurofighter Typhoon and the Sukhoi Su-35S etc., is considered a cost effective counter to so called 'stealth' optimised aircraft (aircraft designed for reduced radar detectability). Detection range is classified, but would certainly extend to several tens of kilometres. Values of ~130-240 km have been postulated, but these values should be treated with caution as they are estimates. The laser system has a range estimated at in excess of ~18 km, but this may extend further or be reduced, with interruptions resulting from adverse environmental conditions (Harkins, 2004).

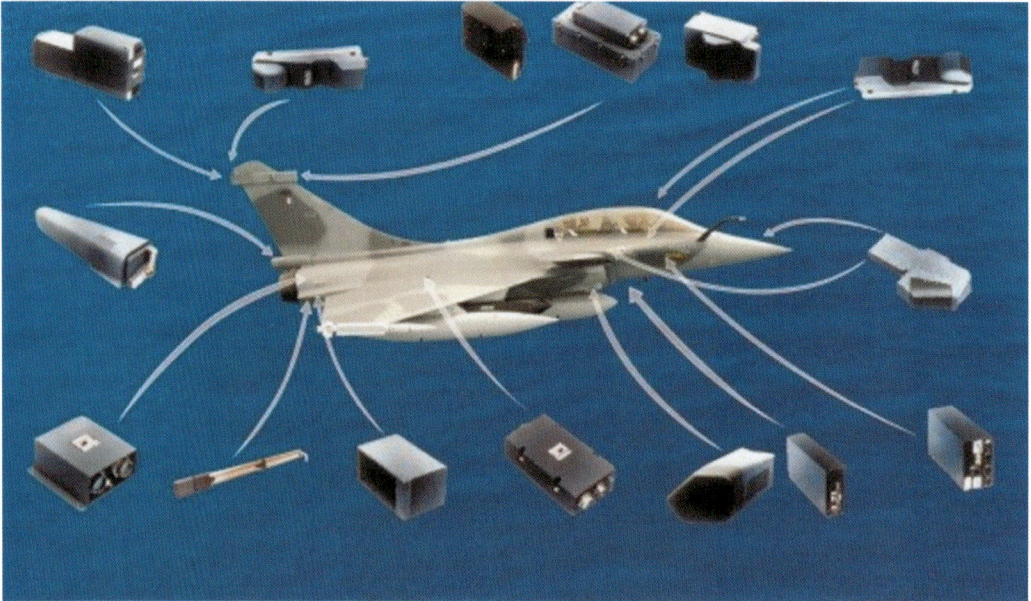

Diagram illustrating the constituent parts of the SPECTRA complex and their respective positioning on the Rafale platform. Thales

SPECTRA – Rafale was equipped with a completely internal electronic warfare and self-defence suite – SPECTRA EW, integrated with the other sensors – radar, FSO etc. SPECTRA, developed by Thales and MBDA (Matra British Aerospace Dynamics Alenia), provisioned for 360° long-range target detection and identification, accurate localisation and action modes in laser, infrared and electro-magnetic spectrums (Thales, MBDA, 2015 & MBDA, 2011). This multi-spectra system incorporates a suite of advanced sensor/decoy technologies – radar, laser and missile warning receivers to detect threats, a phased-array radar jamming system and decoy dispenser system to counter threats to the host aircraft – for RF (Radio Frequency) detection, laser detection (warning), infrared detection, multi-threat RF high power jamming, decoy deployment and a threat warning display. The RF detection capability provides the ability to detect and identify threats at long-range with accurate direction finding. The laser detection system provides both laser warning detection and direction finding against 'last generation threats' (Thales). The infrared detection system provides a passive missile warning capability for defence against both air to air and air to surface missile threats. The multi-threat RF high power jamming capability incorporated modern technology advances and integrated 'multi DRFM' [Digital Radio Frequency Measures] and solid state transmitters' (Thales). The decoy system could include IR/EM/EO (Infrared/Electromagnetic/Electro-optical) ejection cartridges and a battery of chaff ejection tubes. SPECTRA also incorporated a management system for reaction decisions against threats, and data-fusion exploited sensors for display on 2D or 3D localisation on the threat warning display (JEWC, MBDA, 2015 & MBDA, 2011). MBDA developed the DDM (later DDM-NG) infrared MWS (Missile Warning System), the data management system and threat dispensing suite capable of smart multi-dispensing function (MBDA, 2015 & MBDA, 2011).

The SPECTRA RF detection sensor is located on the Rafale engine trunks (here just below the red test flight markings) and the laser detection sensor is located on the canard pivot shoulder leading edge surface. Author

Previous page top: The Multi-threat RF High Power Jammer is located at the base of the vertical tail surface, facing rearward. Previous page bottom and this page: The infrared detection sensor is located on the upper vertical tail surface. Safran-Eric Drouin/DGA Cazaux

Antennas for SPECTRA are mounted in extensions on the forward part of Rafale canard fore-planes, on a pod on the upper vertical tail surface, at the base of the vertical tail surface, on the fuselage, port and starboard, and a battery of four upward-firing launchers for chaff/flare decoys is designed into the airframe (Thales).

Development of SPECTRA had commenced in 1989 and a prototype system was delivered in 1993. Trials in a Dassault Mystere 20 laboratory commenced in October 1994. Rafale M02 and B01 were equipped with SPECTRA in 1996 for integration trials with other sensors, radar etc. (Thales & Harkins, 2004). A basic SPECTRA capability was available for the F1 Standard Rafale, with improved capability introduced with subsequent F2 and F3 Standards (Harkins, 2004).

Among the most advanced 4th/4th+ airborne platform self-defence suites, SPECTRA provides the ability to accurately locate surface based threats so that they could be avoided (Dassault, 2020). This, of course, would be increasingly difficult with advanced capability long range air defence systems emerging, including Russian S-400 and S-500, designed to overcome the threat from 4th+ and 5th generation combat aircraft.

A salvo of decoy flares is launched from the SPECTRA upward firing launchers designed into the Rafale airframe. SIRPA Air-Paringaux-Ravenel

DAMOCLES – DAMOCLES is a multifunctional pod system that combines laser designation, reconnaissance, ground attack and FLIR (Forward Looking Infrared) functions. The pod system was intended for the guidance of smart munitions in day/night conditions and was also outfitted with a sensor suite to provision a navigation and air to air target identification capability. DAMOCLES was cleared for operation from a number of airborne platforms, including Rafale (Thales, 2016 & Thales, 2014).

For operations in an air to surface role DAMOCLES was developed to be interoperable with laser guided, INS/GPS (Inertial Navigation System/Global Positioning System) guided and imagery (television) guided air launched bombs/missiles. DAMOCLES was optimised for use in autonomous or cooperative modes, employing integrated laser spot tracking and laser marker to designate targets, which are recognised by the integral sensors with 3D localisation. Post-strike, DAMOCLES could conduct damage assessment at long-range. DAMOCLES could also be used in an integrated navigation function, courtesy of the integral FLIR, and could be employed as a reconnaissance asset in day/night light conditions. In the air to air role DAMOCLES provided visual target identification (Thales, 2016 & Thales, 2014).

Previous page top: DAMOCLES multifunctional designation, navigation and reconnaissance pod system (top) and **DAMOCLES** displayed alongside **Rafale B01 at Farnborough in 1998 (bottom). This page: DAMOCLES** carried on the starboard forward fuselage shoulder station of a serial Rafale. Author/Dassault Aviation

DAMOCLES technical characteristics – data furnished by Thales Group

Imagery
Third generation detector
Spectral band: 3-5 μm
Field of view: Wide field of view, 4° x 3°; Narrow field of view, 1° x 0.75° and Electronic magnification, x 2
Laser range finding (Eye Safe)
Wavelength: 1.5 μm
Laser designation
Wavelength: 1.06 μm
STANAG 3733
Laser spot tracker
Wavelength: 1.06 μm
Laser marker
Wavelength: 0.8 μm

DAMOCLES would be supplanted in service by the TALIOS third generation omnirole optronics pod system shown on the starboard forward fuselage shoulder station of a Rafale. Thales

TALIOS – DAMOCLES was set to be superseded by the new generation TALIOS (Targeting Long-range Identification System), a third generation omnirole optronics pod system. TALIOS, which was in qualitative and quantitate service with Rafale units of the French Navy and Air Force in 2019, is optimised to produce HD (High Definition) colour data through infrared and visible spectrum sensors, a capability in advance of that available with DAMOCLES. TALIOS improved on operator situation awareness and featured an automatic target detection and recognition capability courtesy of artificial intelligence technology incorporated into the design (Thales, 2019). The system can detect and track fixed location and moving targets, facilitated by installed algorithms (Thales, 2019).

For operations in an air to surface role TALIOS is interoperable with laser guided, INS/GPS guided and imagery (television) guided air launched bombs/missiles. The pod was optimised for use in autonomous or cooperative modes, employing integrated laser spot tracking and a laser marker to designate targets, which were recognised by the integral sensors with 3D localisation. Post-strike, TALIOS could be employed for damage assessment at long-range. As with DAMOCLES, TALIOS could also be used in an integrated navigation function, courtesy of the FLIR, and could be utilised as a dual-band reconnaissance asset capable of operations in day/night light conditions. In the air to air role TALIOS provided identification of airborne targets in day/night light conditions (Thales, 2019).

Imagery taken from TALIOS sensor of a tactical ground layout with the armoured vehicles, located in the bottom right hand corner, magnified and superimposed on the centre of the image. Thales

TALIOS was developed to advance on DAMOCLES capability based on data obtained from operation of the latter system. Advantages over DAMOCLES include incorporation of a cooperative bi-directional data-link for the exchange of data with other sensors, a target recognition function and the capability for positive identification when operating in complex operational environments. TALIOS also added a very wide field of view to the system capabilities – DAMOCLES operated in wide and narrow field of views only (Thales, 2019).

TALIOS technical characteristics – data furnished by Thales Group

IR Imagery
Continuous electronic zoom: 4.8° to 0.12°
Spectral band: 3-5 μm
Field of view: Very Wide field of view, 24° x 18°; Wide field of view, 4.8° x 3.6°; Narrow field of view, 1° x 0.7° and Electronic magnification, x 2
Television Imagery
Continuous electronic zoom: 7.0° to 0.06° (with PiP)
Spectral band: 0.35 μm to 0.7 μm & 0.7 μm to 0.9 μm
Field of view: from 0.77° x 0.58° to 7° x 5.5°
Laser Range Finding (Eye-safe)
Wavelength: 1.5 μm
Laser designation
Wavelength: 1.06 μm
STANAG 3733
Laser spot tracker
Wavelength: 1.06 μm
STANAG 3733
Laser marker
Wavelength: 0.8 μm
Recording/In-flight replay
Multichannel HD digital recorder
AIRNC-8 18 Digital video output

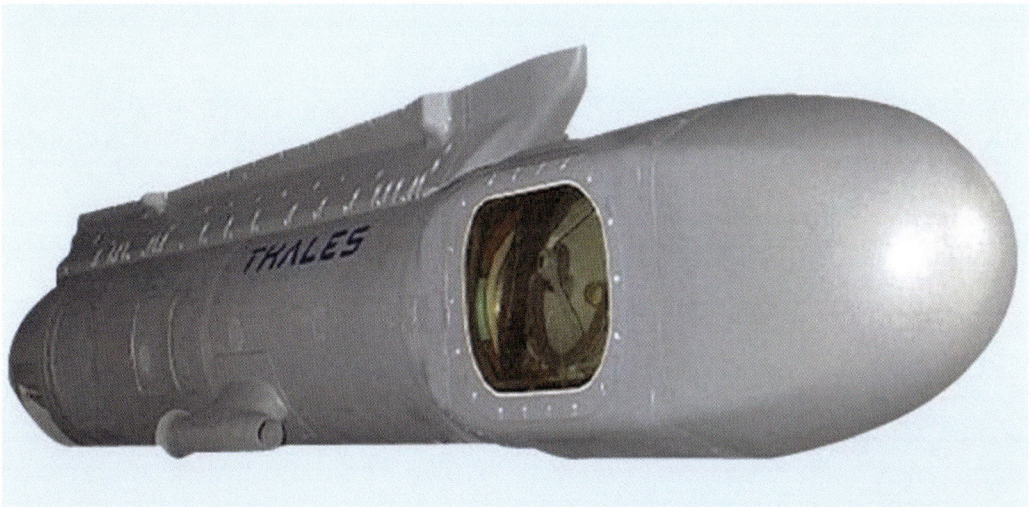

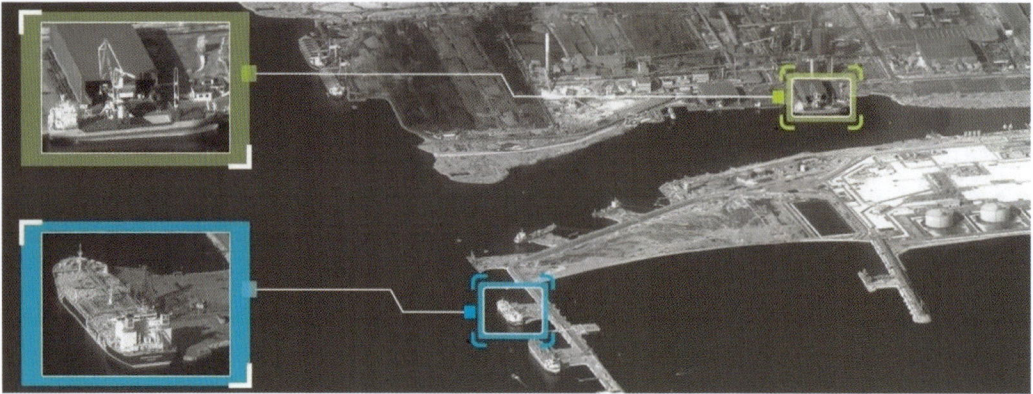

The Thales AREOS (Airborne Reconnaissance Observation System) operated by Rafale (previous page) and imagery of port facilities and vessels taken by AREOS with magnification shown in insets. Thales

AREOS – The AREOS (Airborne Reconnaissance Observation System) was developed for Rafale as a day/night IMINT (Image Intelligence) asset for operations in environmental conditions of fair/adverse weather. AREOS facilitated an IMINT capability, whereby the system would detect, observe and identify a target area at long range when the carrier platform (Rafale) was operating in a high speed/low altitude flight environment. The system would reduce the time required, over that extant for legacy systems, in the sensor data acquisition to target engagement process (Thales, 2016b & Thales, 2013b).

The AREOS (formerly Recco NG) system consisted of three basic airborne and surface based modules – Mission planning software, Mobile surface antenna terminal and a Ground Image Exploitation Station. The system was optimised for automatic imagery collection and transfer via high-speed datalink. The 2 x mobile antennas enabled transmission of 'high rate image data within the optical range (350 km)' and a service link antenna could track and monitor the AREOS pod (Thales, 2016b & Thales, 2013b). Negation of the requirement for radio communication enhanced operation of the AREOS system by reducing potential for misinterpretations and speed up the process of target detection and decision making to act on target information and implementation of the action to be taken (Thales, 2016b). The image collection suite consisted of 2 x wide focal plane arrays for generation of visible and infrared spectrum image data, featuring synchronous dual-band collection of said data (Thales, 2016b). The main optics operated in 2 fields, including telescopic, and facilitated continuous views in high resolution at long stand-off range from the carrier platform. A high-speed infrared line-scanner enabled panoramic acquisition when operating at very low altitudes (Thales, 2016b).

Acquisition of AREOS for deployment in Rafale bestowed upon France a high performance tactical/quasi-strategic (with forward deployment, aircraft carrier deployment and or in-flight refueling) optronics reconnaissance capability. This provided command with high quality situational awareness of areas of interest, such as potential targets and adversary asset dispositions. AREOS, connected to the overall C4ISR (Command Control Communication Computer Intelligence Surveillance Reconnaissance) network, was operational on the F3 Standard Rafale in service with the French Air Force and Navy (Thales, 2016b).

The Rafale M trialed the AREOS (Recco NG) pod. Thales

MAINTENANCE REDUCTION – Reducing Rafale maintenance demands and costs was a major programme requirement. To this end, Rafale servicing/maintenance is accomplished at operational base locations – there is no requirement for the aircraft to be shipped to depots for airframe/engine inspections as was the case with previous generation combat aircraft – SRU (Shop [workshop] Replaceable Units) are the only elements that required depot level maintenance (Dassault, 2020).

The M88 engine is a modular design – twenty one modules (as noted above). For maintenance/repair, each individual module, or a particular engine part, can be removed and dispatched to a repair depot or the manufacture depot. A replacement module could be installed and the engine made ready for operation with no requirement for engine run tests (Dassault, 2020).

Overall Rafale mission failure rate was reduced not only through new technologies, but through omission of systems/aerodynamic surfaces that were prone to failures in previous generation aircraft, thereby reducing the spare parts inventory that would have to be stocked by operators. To this end, Rafale has no dedicated airbrake, engine air intakes have no moving parts and AC generators lack a constant speed drive. Dassault credits the decision of having a fixed refuelling probe rather than a retractable in-flight refuelling probe as being to eliminate the potential for failure of the system during deployment and retraction (Dassault, 2020). Another area where the fixed probe has advantage over the retractable probe found on contemporary designs, is a reduction in empty weight. The fixed probe advantage over a retractable probe system is, of course, a contentious point as the fixed refuelling probe, whilst having obvious advantages in that its lack of complexity reduced the potential for failures, had equally obvious drawbacks – increased aerodynamic drag and slight increase in radar signature being but two.

The fixed in-flight refuelling probe on Rafale starboard forward fuselage reduces maintenance requirements and failures. Author

Further parts inventory/maintenance reduction efforts were present in the standardisation approach – for instance parts for canard foreplane or the FCS actuators, where possible, were standardised in that the same parts were utilised for port or starboard (Dassault, 2020). Sensor/electronic systems, such as radar, SPECTRA and MDPU, maintenance is reduced through the concept of Line Replaceable Units – LRU. This concept is extended further through replacement of circuit boards within the respective LRU (Dassault, 2020). The side opening canopy provisions for increased ease of removal of the crew ejection seat(s) – a single ejection seat can be removed in 10 minutes by two ground technicians (Dassault, 2020). Anti-corrosion maintenance measures were also reduced over legacy designs, such as the Dassault Super Etendard.

In the early 2000's, Rafale B01 was trial fitted with upper fuselage conformal fuel tank aerodynamic shapes. This configuration, which was not adopted for service, would have increased overall fuel capacity, but at the expense of increased weight and potentially reduced stores carriage capacity. Author

At the dawn of the third decade of the twenty first century the F3 Standard Rafale (bottom) – Rafale M27 shown configured with an AM 39 Exocet anti-ship cruise missile – was a quantum leap in capability over the interim F1 Standard (top) introduced to service in 2004. USN/Marine National

Rafale B (foreground) configured for an air to surface mission and Rafale C (background) configured for an air defence mission. Dassault Aviation-K. Tokunaga

Enhancements to the Rafale F3 Standard saw new aircraft delivered from 2012 to F3-04T Standard, equipped with the AESA RBE2 radar complex, a new missile launch detector and an enhanced capability – in the areas of target detection and identification – FSO, designated FSO-IT (Dassault, 2020). Further research and development work continued in various areas, including enhancing air to air and air to surface capability and overall sensor functionality in order to increase potential for viable detection, tracking and identification of target sets in the face of countermeasures. Survivability of the overall Rafale platform would be enhanced through addition of low-observable radar modes and enhancements to the SPECTRA EW complex. These enhancements to capability would feed into the F-3R Standard.

The F4 Standard Rafale development contract was placed on 14 January 2019. Key enhancements of the F4 Standard, which would build on the F3-04T and F3-R Standards, included further enhancing the platforms network centric capability through incorporation of 'new satellite and intra-patrol links', modern communications server and 'software defined radio)' (Dassault). In addition, the AESA RBE2 and

FSO were planned to be updated and new helmet-mounted display capabilities were to be introduced. Planned enhancements to the Rafale weapon capability included addition of MICA NG (Next Generation) air to air missile and addition of the 1000 kg AASM precision guided air to surface munition. The F4 Standard initial development was scheduled for completion in 2024, although data available from Dassault in 2020 suggested that some of the enhancements may be available several years earlier (Dassault, 2020).

In 2020, the F4 Standard Rafale was considered essential to keeping the Rafale a viable platform over the next few decades of service in the face of advanced potential adversary platforms of the 4++, 5th and potentially 6th generations.

Rafale specification – data furnished by Dassault Aviation

Dimensions
    Wing span: 10.90 m
    Length: 15.30 m
    Height: 5.30 m
Overall empty weight: 10 tonne (10000 kg class)
Maximum take-off weight: 24.5 tonne (24500 kg class)
External fuel load: 4.7 tonne (4700 kg)
External load: up to 6.7 tonne (6700 kg)
Stores stations: 14 on Rafale B/C and 13 on Rafale M
Wet stores stations for external fuel carriage: 5 heavy stations
Engines: 2 x M88-2 afterburning turbofans, each rated at ~7.82 tonne (7.7 ton) thrust
Load limits: -3.2 g/+9 g
Maximum speed: Mach 1.8*
Service ceiling: 15240 m (50,000 ft.)*
Approach speed: under 222 km/h (~120 knots)
Landing run: 450 m without employment of drag parachute

*Some Dassault documentation credits the Rafale with the ability to reach a speed of Mach 2 and an altitude of 16764 m (55,000 ft.) (Dassault AR, 2005)

4

ADVANCED WEAPON PLATFORM

The design of the Dassault Rafale weapon system was centred around the ability to deploy a large diversity of guided and unguided air to air and air to surface weapons, carried externally, as well as the incorporation of a fixed cannon armament, housed internally. Total external stores load was in the range of 9072 kg. The stores management system was centred on a MIL-STD-1760 compliant data-bus, allowing integration of advanced air to air and air to surface weapons as they became available.

Stores could be carried on fourteen stores stations (thirteen in the Rafale M), which include eight wing stations – 2 x inner wing, 2 x intermediate (inner intermediate), 2 x outer (outer intermediate) and 2 x wingtip – the balance being located on the fuselage – fuselage shoulder and fuselage centre stations. Five of the external stores stations were designed wet, allowing a large external fuel load to be carried in up to five 2000 litre subsonic flight capable external fuel tanks, or up to five 1250 litre supersonic flight capable external fuel tanks, or an asymmetric mixture of both types (Harkins, 2004).

Rafale fixed armament consisted of a single GIAT Industries (NEXTER) M791 30 mm cannon (housed in the aircraft fuselage), capable of firing at up to 2500 rounds per minute. In the Rafale A technology demonstrator, the cannon housing was located in the port forward fuselage section. In the serial Rafale B/C/M, the cannon housing was relocated to the lower section of the starboard engine duct, with the muzzle opening located at the starboard wing root – 125 rounds of 30 mm ammunition could be accommodated (Harkins, 2004).

Top: Rafale M01 exhibited in 1996 with a plethora of extant and proposed stores. From right to left: MICA IR; MICA EM; BGL 1000 kg laser guided bomb; APACHE; designation pod; M791 30 mm cannon; ANNG ; AM 39; AS 30; AASM and Magic II. Bottom: Rafale B01 exhibited in 1998 with then planned or proposed stores. From right to left: MICA IR; MICA EM; Magic II; PGM; SCALP EG; ANF; DAMOCLES; CLB8; M791 cannon; fuel tank; AASM etc. Much of these stores options were not adopted. Author

The gas-powered 30 M791 30 mm cannon, which weighed in at ~120 kg, is a seven-chamber revolver cannon with a very high rate of fire – a twenty one round burst can apparently be fired in a time of ~0.5 seconds – with velocity in the region of 1025 m/s, increasing hit probability against airborne targets (assuming accurate aiming). Effective range against airborne targets is in the region of 2500 m. The M791 could fire several types of round and was equipped with a pyrotechnic rearming system for the rejection of faulty rounds. Following development and trials, the M791 was cleared for operation on the Rafale in 2001 (Harkins, 2004).

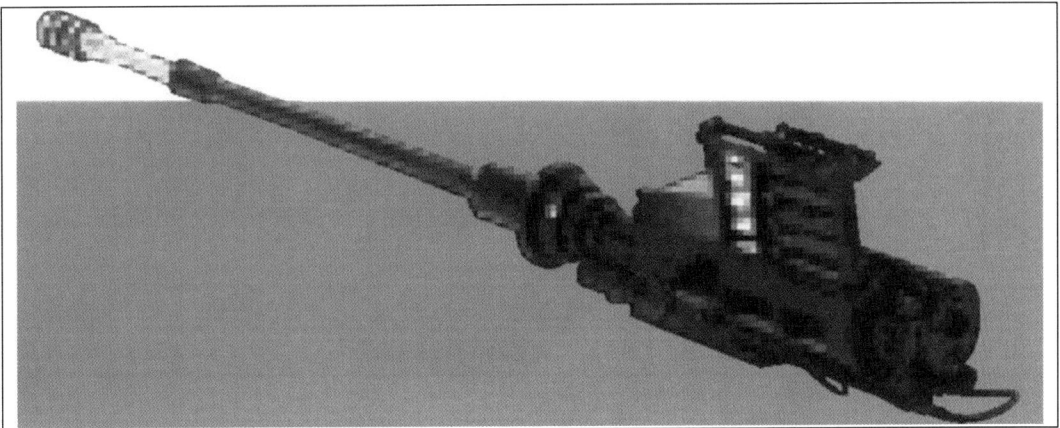

30 M791 automatic cannon. GIAT

MICA – The Rafale primary air to air missile armament consist of the MBDA (MATRA BAe Dynamics Alenia) MICA (*Missile d'Interception de Combat et d' Autodéfence*. This was developed with two interchangeable seeker heads on a common missile airframe – MICA IR (Infrared) passive dual waveband IIR (Imaging Infrared) – heat seeking – and MICA EM RF (Radio Frequency) active radar seeker, offering shoot up/shoot down capability. MICA IR is guided by the Sagem (Safran Group) developed MICA IR passive IIR homing head sensor (capable of discriminating against the target and deployed countermeasures) (Safran) and MICA EM was guided by a Thales AD4A active radar seeker head, apparently operating in the J band (Harkins, 2004).

MICA can be described as a BVR (Beyond Visual Range) capable system for multi-launch/guide against multiple targets, featuring enhanced performance in short-range engagements. MICA has demonstrated high performance in short/long range operation. For short-range combat MICA featured a lock-on after launch mode, with high performance in acquisition and tracking, 360° missile launch envelope and general performance pushing toward a goal of the first shot/first kill principle in all spheres (MBDA, 2015 & MBDA, 2011) – a trait more or less universally claimed by modern missile designers.

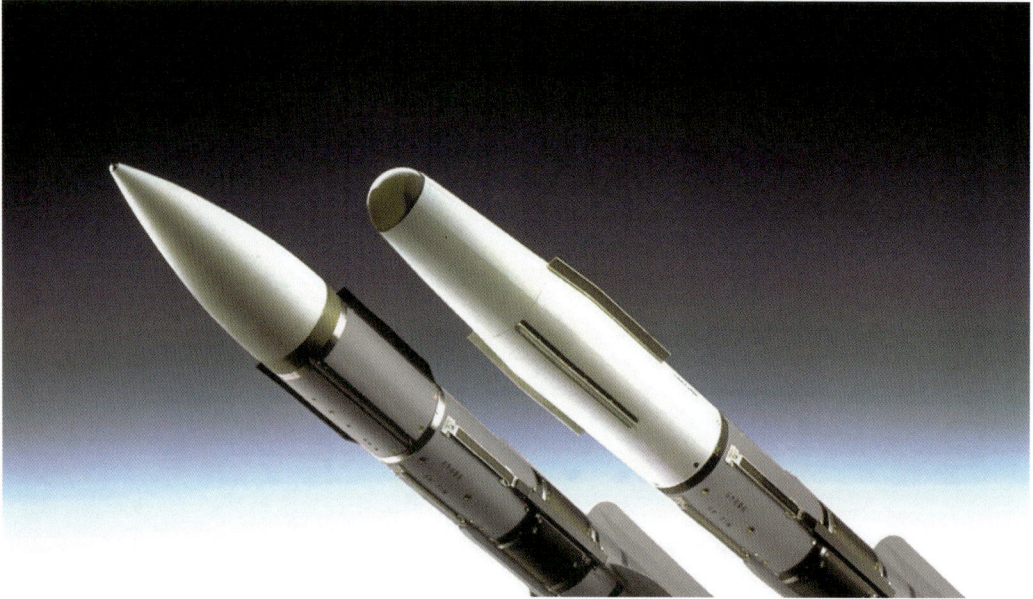

Top: MICA EM (left of image) and MICA IR front sections. Bottom: MICA IR and MICA EM air to air missiles. MBDA/Author

Top: **A MICA air to air missile is launched from a Rafale M development aircraft during development/integration trials. Bottom: Serial Rafale C armed with 4 x MICA EM, 2 x MICA IR and a 1250 litre external fuel tank.** MBDA/*Armée de l'Air*-O. Ravenel

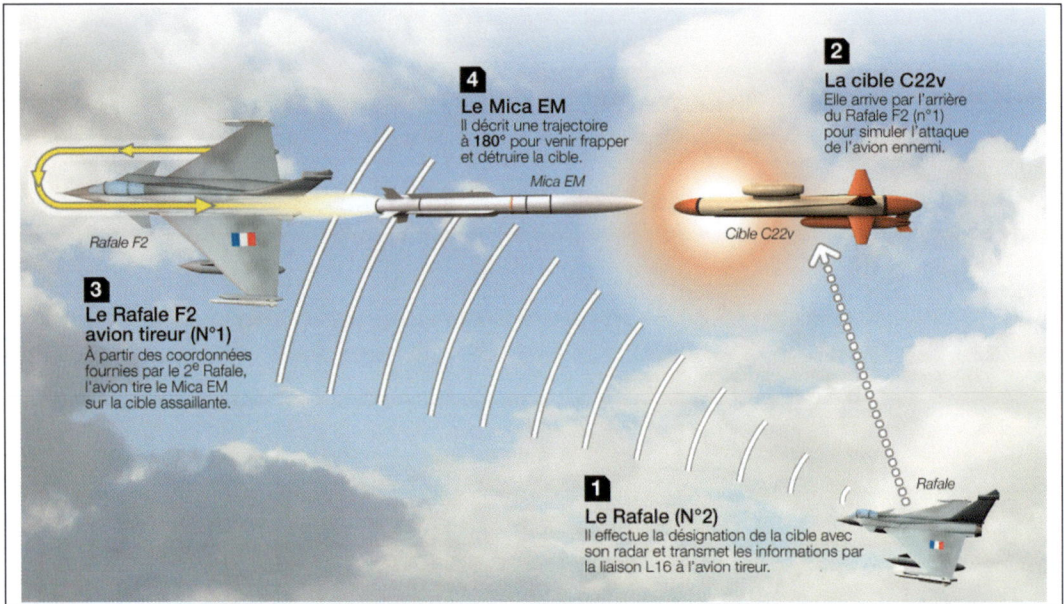

Top: Graphic depicting F2 Standard Rafale engaging a target in the rear hemisphere with MICA EM: 1. Rafale No.2 designates the target with its radar then transmits the data via the L (Link) 16 data-link; 2. The C22v target drone arrives in rear hemisphere of Rafale F2 (No.1), simulating an enemy aircraft. 3. Rafale F2 aircraft No.1, employing coordinate data transmitted from Rafale No.2, launches a MICA EM at the C22v target in the rear hemisphere. 4. The MICA EM flies a 180° turn to engage and destroy the target. Bottom: Although predominantly associated with the MICA IR, the MICA EM can be carried on and launched from the wingtip launch rails, demonstrated by **Rafale M1.** Studio V2-MBDA/MBDA

French marine Rafale M21 (top) and M18 (bottom) during training operations from a USN aircraft carrier during 22-23 July 2008, with vacant wingtip missile launch rails on M21 and wingtip mounted **MICA IR** missiles on **M18** USN

MICA IR on the port wingtip station of a Rafale M. MBDA

When launched on medium or long-range engagements the active-radar guided MICA EM employed strap-down inertial guidance, which, if required, could be updated via a data-link from the launch aircraft during long range engagements. The missiles on-board active radar seeker head would only be activated during the terminal phase of the engagement. For short-range engagements the missile is locked on to the target prior to launching. The MICA IR variant, which is the longest-range weapon of its type in the western world, could also be employed for passive IR monitoring during the mission, complementing the active monitoring of the AESA RBE2 radar (Harkins, 2004).

Powered by a high impulse low smoke emitting solid propellant rocket motor, MICA would cruise and manoeuvre toward the target – speed is classified, but is thought to be around Mach 4 – under aerodynamic/control – elongated main wings, tail control surfaces and thrust vector control for exhaust forces. Lock on to the target would occur either prior to launch or after launch when engaging long-range targets or against targets initially designated by another Rafale. The blast-fragmentation warhead is activated by either RF proximity or impact fuse and the target is destroyed/disabled by directed splinters (MBDA, 2015 & MBDA, 2011).

MICA IR carried on the starboard wingtip station of a Rafale M. MBDA

Design of MICA, which has a launch weight of 112 kg; length, 3.1 m; span, 56 cm and diameter, 16 cm, had commenced at MATRA in 1975. The new missile design was to be developed as both a BVR and close range missile able to replace legacy MATRA R.530 (semi-active radar homing) and R.550 (infrared homing) missiles arming then planned Mirage 2000/4000 generation aircraft. Full-scale development commenced in 1987 and flight test of aerodynamic missile shapes commenced in 1994. A MICA IR equipped with an imaging IIR guidance system was flight tested on a Mirage 2000 the following year. Initial development was completed in 1997, paving the way for introduction to service on French Air Force Mirage 2000-5F serving with 1/2 'Cigognes' and 2/2 'Cote d'Ore'. Integration of the MICA EM on the F1 Standard Rafale was completed in summer 2000. This trial phase had included the first guided firing of MICA from a Rafale in June 1995; inertial guided firing of MICA in May 1997; deployment of a MICA EM missile, using an ejector launch, against a supersonic target drone at the Landes test range in June 1997 and multi-target inertial guided firing of MICA air to air missiles in an electronic warfare environment, with target position updates via the aircraft to missile datalink, in November 1997. The MICA EM received initial qualification for employment on the Rafale in June 1998 (Harkins, 2004).

MICA – data furnished by MBDA

Weight: 112 kg
Length: 3.1 m
Diameter: 160 mm
Homing heads: Active, MICA EM or passive imaging infrared, MICA IR
Thrust vector control system
Rail and ejection launch

In 2018, development of MICA NG was authorised. This next generation MICA, with interchangeable seeker heads (increased sensitivity IR matrix and AESA) and extended range, is intended to replace MICA EM/IR with deliveries scheduled for 2026 (Dassault, 2018).

The original Rafale concept included the R.550 Magic II short-range IR guided air to air missile as an armament option – armed F1 Standard Rafale M, which entered service with the French Navy in 2004. Rafale M02 development aircraft is shown with an R.550 on the starboard wingtip station during aircraft carrier deck trials. Dassault Aviation

MAGIC II – Whilst an IR guided variant of the MICA was developed for BVR/short range engagements of airborne targets, the previous generation MATRA (MBDA) R.550 Magic II was employed during development and early service and remained operational on the Super Etendard *Modernise* strike fighter (Harkins, 2004), retired in 2016 (Dassault).

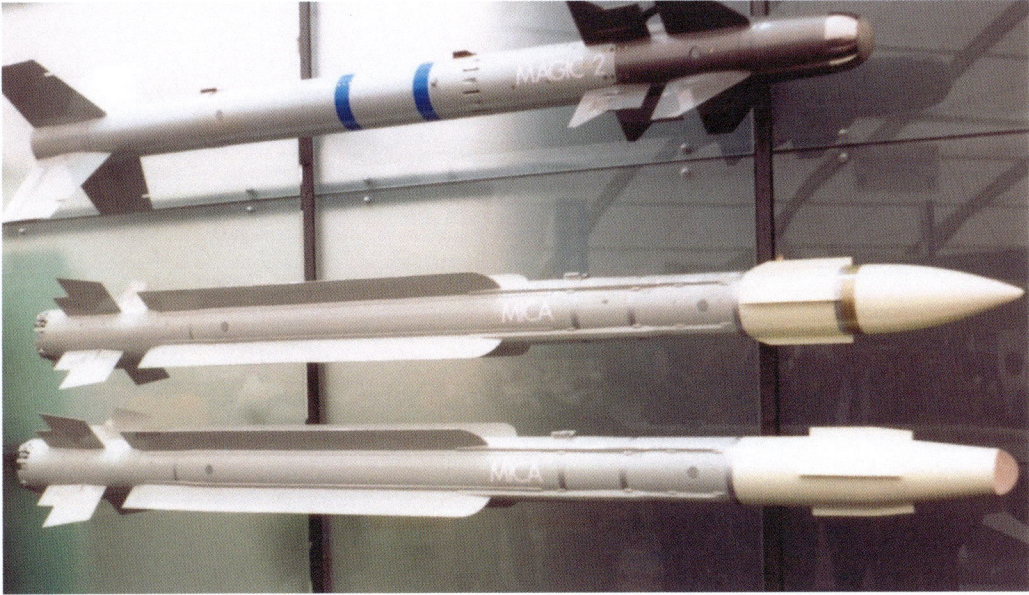

MICA IR (centre of photograph) superseded the R.550 (top of photograph) with the introduction of the F2 and F3 Standard Rafale in 2006 and 2008 respectively. Author

R.550 Magic II – data furnished by MBDA

Length: 2.75 m
Diameter: 0.16 m
Weight: 89 kg
Speed: Mach 2.7
Range: around 13
Warhead: 12.5 kg high explosive blast fragmentation
Fuse: Radio Frequency proximity
Guidance: infrared seeker with all-aspect engagement capability

METEOR – MICA has been credited with a range of around 60 km. However, the design was not considered to be capable of extending range to that required for the emerging extended beyond visual range mission formulated in the mid-1990's. In the late 1990's, the main driving force behind European and US BVRAAM (Beyond Visual Range Air to Air Missile) development work was primarily aimed at meeting a British requirement, SR(A)1239 (Staff Requirement Air 1239), to arm Eurofighter Typhoon. Through a plethora of twists and turns this emerged as the MBDA Meteor.

The UK BVRAAM competition was only the first of a number of European competitions to meet similar requirements. The remaining Eurofighter partner nations, Germany, Italy and Spain, as well as Sweden and France, all required an extended range BVRAAM for Typhoon, Saab JAS 39 Gripen and Rafale respectively. The European consortium competing for the UK (United Kingdom) contract pointed out that Meteor was essential to Europe retaining control over export of its combat aircraft, which, if armed with US (United States) missiles, would be subject to US Congressional approval for export sales. This argument won through when the UK selected Meteor in June 2000 – MBDA was selected as prime-contractor for the European program and the UK and Sweden provided development approval in June 2001 (Harkins, 2013, Harkins, 2004, Harkins, 2004a & Harkins 1997). The Meteor consortium would encompass a number of European companies to meet the BVRAAM requirements of the six partner nations – UK, Sweden, Germany, Italy, Spain and France (MBDA, 2018) – as the primary air to air armament for Typhoon, Gripen and Rafale combat aircraft, as well as projected new combat aircraft, such as the Lockheed Martin F-35 in UK service.

Artist rendering of Rafale B01 launching a Meteor extended range air to air missile from the starboard shoulder stores station. MBDA

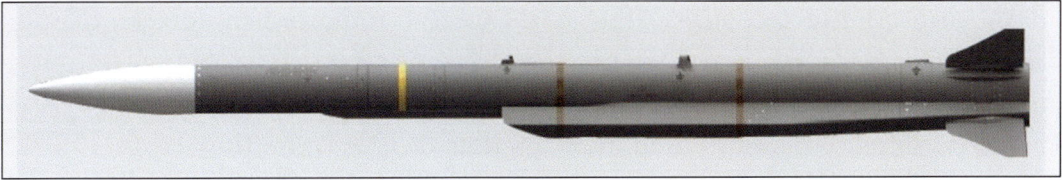

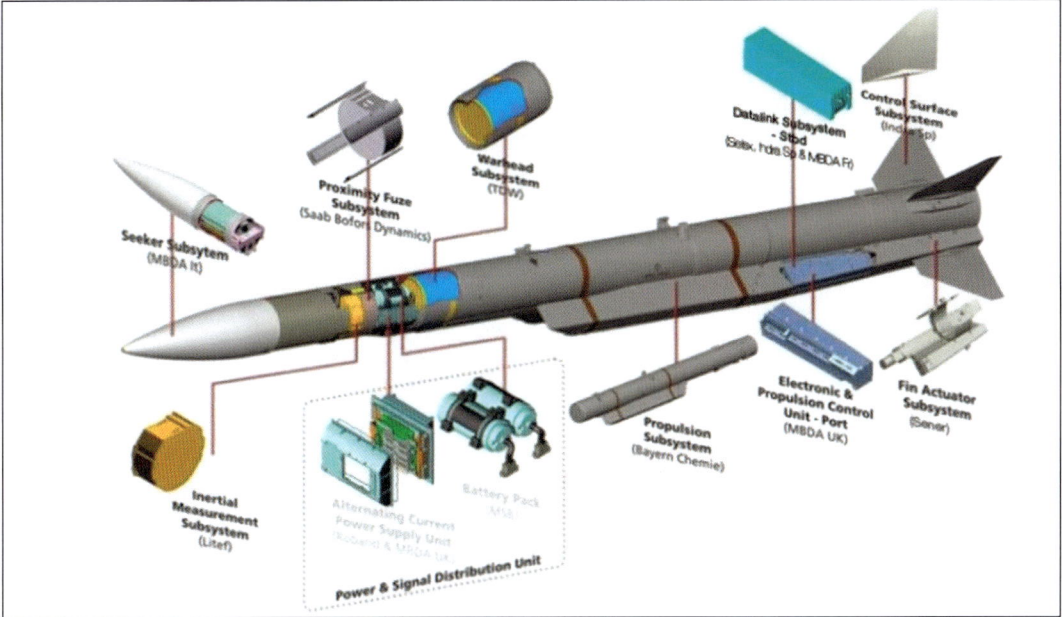

Profile diagrammatic view of Meteor (top) and a diagrammatic view of Meteor with a breakdown of the missile constituent parts (bottom). MBDA

On 23 December 2002, the UK signed the Meteor development contract (in effect, the development launch for all six partner nations). The following year the design evolution moved from a winged to a wingless configuration, which was trial fitted to a Typhoon that same year, followed the following year by trial fit to a Gripen and a Rafale (MBDA, 2011).

Meteor handling characteristics was trialled on Rafale during a series of catapult assisted take-off and landings of a Rafale M operating from the aircraft carrier *Charles de Gaulle* in 2005. Development progress that same year involved flight testing Meteor representative aerodynamic bodies on Typhoon, Gripen and Rafale aircraft (MBDA, 2011). Meteor Test firings had commenced in 2006, when a series of Meteor firings below medium altitudes were conducted from a Gripen (MBDA, 2013). In early July 2012, MBDA concluded Meteor guided firing trials with three successful launches, each achieving direct hits against targets deploying countermeasures. The trials were conducted under electronic protection measures aimed at proving Meteor's capability against targets in a near operational environment (MBDA, 2013 & Harkins, 2013). A Meteor missile was launched from Rafale B301, operating from DGA (*Délégué Général pour l'armament*) Cazaux, in October 2012 – notification had been issued for the Tranche 1 contract covering Meteor integration on Rafale in 2011 – as France progressed toward increasing Rafale capabilities through the F3-R program launched in December that year ((Dassault AR, 2011 & Dassault AR, 2012).

In 2018, Meteor was serving with the Swedish Gripen and was on the cusp of entering service with the Eurofighter Typhoon fleets of the UK, Germany, Italy, Spain and Rafale in service in France (MBDA, 2018).

Meteor missile on the starboard intermediate wing station during development/integration on Rafael M1. Dassault Aviation

Meteor is made up of a number of subsystems: Seeker subsystem (MBDA It); Proximity fuse subsystem (Saab Bofors Dynamics); Warhead subsystem (TDW); Inertial measurement subsystem (Litef); Power & Signal distribution unit – Alternating current power supply unit (Roband & MBDA UK) & Battery pack (MSB) – Propulsion subsystem (Bayern Chemie); Datalink subsystem – starboard, Electronic &

propulsion control unit-port (MBDA UK); Control surface subsystem & Fin actuator subsystem (Sener) (MBDA, 2013).

Rafale M1 take-off (top) and during flight trials (bottom) with Meteor missiles on the fuselage shoulder and wing intermediate stations. Dassault Aviation/MBDA-Thierry Wurtz

Top: Rafale M configured with a Meteor missile on the starboard intermediate station and a 1250 litre external fuel tank on the starboard inner wing station. Bottom: Rafale M configured with Meteor missiles on the starboard fuselage shoulder and wing intermediate stations. MBDA

Top: Rafale with instrumented/camera systems for recording Meteor development launches. Meteor missiles are carried on the fuselage shoulder stations – the starboard missile is adorned with calibration markings. Bottom: A calibrated Meteor missile is ejected from a Rafale fuselage station – note the extended ejector jacks (arms). DGA

Meteor was designed to operate effectively in all operational environments. Once launched, Meteor's integral active radar seeker guides the missile to the target in environmental conditions of fair or adverse weather. The inherent network centric (network-enabled) capability provisioned for Meteor operation based on targeting data provided by third party assets, vastly increasing the weapons flexibility of operation (MBDA, 2018). At the heart of the Meteor concept was the extended no escape zone – as of 2020 the largest no escape zone of any in service air to air missile (this would be better described as a reduced probability of escape zone) – described by MBDA as being several times in excess of that of legacy BVRAAM, such as MICA EM. The extended no escape zone is facilitated through the thrust generated by the solid fuel, variable flow ducted rocket propulsion unit. This allowed for Meteor high speed (throttleable) to be maintained all the way to the target, even when employed on long range engagements (MBDA, 2018 & MBDA, 2013a). This alleviated a deficiency in previous generation BVRAAM in that speed invariably dropped off as energy was depleted through mechanics/physics of aerodynamic manoeuvring etc. The target would be destroyed or disabled by a blast fragmentation warhead, activated by proximity or impact fuses (MBDA, 2018 & Harkins, 2013a).

Rafale is capable of carrying up to four Meteor missiles, which would normally be carried on the intermediate wing stores stations and on the rear lateral fuselage shoulder stations. Rafale can operate with Meteor and MICA in both EM and IR variants (MBDA).

Meteor – data furnished by MBDA (2018, 2015 & 2011)

Weight: 190 kg
Length: 3.7 m
Diameter: 178 mm
Rail and ejection launch capability
Propulsion: solid fuel variable flow ducted rocket (ramjet)
Seeker: active RF
Navigation and guidance:
    Bank-to-turn manoeuvring
    Inertial mid-course with data-link
    Autonomous terminal guidance employing advanced proportional navigation
Warhead: Blast fragmentation
Fuses: Impact/proximity

Rafale B configured with a single ASMPA nuclear armed stand-off missile, 6 x MICA EM/IR air to air missiles and 2 x 2000 litre subsonic flight capable external fuel tanks. SIRPA Air

A wide diversity of air to surface armament can be carried by the Rafale. These options include the MBDA SCALP EG stand-off cruise missile, the MBDA/Aerospatiale AM 39 Exocet anti-ship missile, and the ASMPA (*Air-Sol Moyenne Portée Amélioré*) nuclear armed stand-off missile, an evolution of the MBDA (formerly Aerospatiale) ASMP (*Air-Sol Moyenne Portée*) medium range nuclear armed stand-off missile – Europe's first operational supersonic air launched cruise missile.

ASMP development had commenced in 1978 and the missile entered service with the French Air Force Dassault Mirage IVP supersonic bomber in 1986, followed by the Mirage 2000N in 1988 and Aeronavale Dassault Super Etendard strike fighter in 1989 (Harkins, 2004).

ASMP was the first service missile in the world powered by a liquid propellant ramjet with integral solid propellant boost motor. The liquid propellant ramjet, designed and manufactured by Aerospatiale (MBDA), was activated once the missile reached a predetermined velocity, achieved by means of the solid-propellant booster integrated with and housed in the ramjet combustion chamber. Under ramjet power the missile speed (classified) was estimated to be around a value of Mach 2 on a low-altitude flight profile, rising to somewhere in the region of Mach 3 on a medium altitude flight profile. Missile range was classified. However, MBDA literature suggests a range of several hundred kilometres on a medium altitude launch, dropping to perhaps 100 km on a low altitude launch. Once released from the launch aircraft the ASMP followed a pre-programmed flight profile employing an inertial reference system to guide it through an extensive flight envelope. The missile was guided by an autonomous inertial navigation system, which afforded the required accuracy. The combination of high-speed and multiple flight profiles for low and medium altitude launch reduced the probability of a successful interception of the missile. The target would have been destroyed by the ~300 kiloton yield TN-80 or TN-81 nuclear warhead developed by what is now the CEA (*Commissariat à l'énergie Atomique*) (Harkins, 2004).

Rafale M01 was exhibited at Farnborough International 1996 with a plethora of weapon options. At the higher end of air to surface capability was the ANNG (innermost to aircraft) which was being studied as a medium-range supersonic air to surface missile (primarily for the anti-ship mission, but potentially for conventional or overland nuclear strike). The ANNG (later ANF) did not progress, but technology was incorporated into the ASMPA program. Author

The **ASMPA** was introduced to service on the **Mirage 2000N** nuclear strike aircraft in 2009, followed by service clearance for operation from the **F3 Standard Rafale** in 2010. MBDA

In late 1994, it emerged that France planned to arm some of its planned Rafale B fleet with the ASMP in the twenty first century as plans were drawn up for operations beyond retirement of the Mirage IVP, the last eight of which were retired from service in 1996. The nuclear strike role was then the preserve of around 45 Mirage 2000N, equipping three squadrons, armed with majority of the 90 serial ASMP manufactured. Plans called for the Rafale B to supplement and eventually supplant the Mirage 2000N in the nuclear strike role armed with ASMP or a replacement missile design (Harkins, 2004) – The Mirage 2000N was retired in June 2018 (Dassault AR, 2018).

A feasibility study for a new generation nuclear armed air launched stand-off missile was launched in 1996. Full program launch occurred toward the end of 1997 and a two-year definition contract was awarded in October 1998. On 29 December 2000, a development contract was awarded to what is now MBDA France. Planning called for service entry on the K3 Standard Mirage 2000N, followed by service entry on the F3 Standard Rafale. To this end, the ASMPA was declared operational on the Mirage 2000N in 2009, followed by operational clearance on the Rafale in 2010 (MBDA, 2015 & French DGA).

Page 138-139: As well as deployment on the Rafale B, ASMPA armed Rafale M of the French Navy, having replaced the ASMP armed Super Etendard. SIRPA Air-Amboise Cyril/Dassault Aviation

The ASMPA (prime contractors: MBDA for air vehicle and CEV for warhead), based on the general architecture of the ASMP, was designed as a successor to the latter design as a medium range air to surface nuclear armed missile with enhanced capabilities in the areas of range; trajectories and penetration, compared with its predecessor. ASMPA, based on the air vehicle developed under the Vesta (ramjet powered air vehicle) program, with design input from the ANF (New Generation Anti-ship Missile) program (cancelled in late 1999), featured improved performance with regard to missile range and reduced radar observability characteristics. ASMPA was powered by a new generation liquid propellant ramjet, with extended combustion time to increase range and provide new flight trajectories. This enhanced the missile capability to penetrate defended airspace. The new propulsion was derived from technology developed for the cancelled ASLP (*Air Sol Longue Portée*) program and the Vesta vector (noted above), under development since 1996. The ramjet facilitated reduced size and weight in relation to mission performance, which, in terms of speed, was stated in MBDA documentation as being high supersonic over a significant portion of the flight envelope. ASMPA utilised new generation navigation/guidance/control equipment (INU (Inertial Navigation Unit), computer etc.) (MBDA, 2015).

The new generation medium energy yield thermo-nuclear warhead arming the ASMPA received operational validation during the last French nuclear test series, and simulations conducted thereafter (MBDA, 2015 & French DGA) – the last test of this series took place on 27 January 1996 at Morurora and Fangataufa Atoll in the South Pacific. Yield of the ASMPA warhead remains classified in 2020, but the yield output of the 27 January 1996 test is estimated at ~120,000 tonnes TNT equivalent (CTBTO, 2011).

The Rafale/ASMPA combination has completely replaced the Mirage 2000N/ASMP/ASMPA in French Air Force service. SIRPA Air-Amboise Cyril

SCALP EG – For medium range conventional strike against fixed location targets, Rafale is armed with the MBDA SCALP EG air launched subsonic cruise missile. From the commencement of the Rafale program it had been advocated that the aircraft would serve as the launch platform for a conventional armed stand-off weapon. Initially this was to be filled by the 140 km range APACHE (*Arme Propulsée À Charges Éjectables*) weapon dispenser, designed as a stand-off missile system. APACHE development had commenced in 1989 and the first qualification firing was successfully conducted in Sweden in August

1997. Germany had become the launch customer for APACHE when it ordered the missile into production as the MAW (Modular Abstandswaffe) in late 1992, Tornado IDS (Interdiction Strike) aircraft being so armed from 1996. In summer 1994, APACHE was launched from a Mirage 2000D and further development testing led to captive carry tests of the weapon on Rafale B01 – missiles were carried on the inboard wing stations. In October 1997, the French DGA ordered 100 APACHE AP, powered by a TRI 60-30 turbojet engine (Safran & Harkins, 2004).

In the early 1990's, the Matra APACHE was expected to form an armament option for Rafale. While this did not come to pass, APACHE would form the basis for the design of the MBDA SCALP EG/Storm Shadow, which entered service in the early 2000's. Author

The APACHE design formed the basis for an evolved variant to meet the British CASOM (Conventionally Armed Stand-Off Missile) requirement to arm the Panavia Tornado GR.4 and Eurofighter Typhoon. This new design became known as Storm Shadow and France adopted a variant referred to as SCALP EG (*Emploi Général*/General Purpose) (Harkins, 2013 & Harkins, 2004).

MATRA APACHE exhibited alongside Rafale M01 at Farnborough in September 1996. Author

While SCALP EG/Storm Shadow shared a similar airframe and the TR 60-30 turbojet propulsion system of APACHE, a number of new systems were incorporated – new guidance/navigation systems, warhead and an additional fuel cell was added to extend range. The TERPROM (Terrain Profile Matching) featured an integrated GPS/INS (Global Positioning System/Inertial Navigation System). GEC Marconi (incorporated into BAE Systems) developed the IIR seeker used in the terminal phase of target engagement for target recognition and acquisition (Harkins, 2013 & Harkins, 2004).

Basic physical characteristics included: weight, 1300 kg; length, 5.10 m and diameter, under 1 m with wings folded and under 3 m with wings deployed. The airframe forward section accommodated electronic equipment and the infrared camera system. The central section accommodated the 907 kg BROACH (Bomb Royal Ordnance Augmented Charge) unitary warhead, the deployable wings and fuel cells and the rear section accommodated the TR 60-30 propulsion unit and rear control surfaces. The fire and forget missile was totally autonomous after launch and can be employed day or night in environmental conditions of fair and adverse weather with IIR homing in the terminal phase of the flight to the target. The missile employed low observable characteristics and a low altitude flight profile to reduce the potential for interception during the flight to target (Harkins, 2013 & Harkins, 2004). Overall range depended on flight profile, but could extend out to in excess of 250 km (MBDA, 2019).

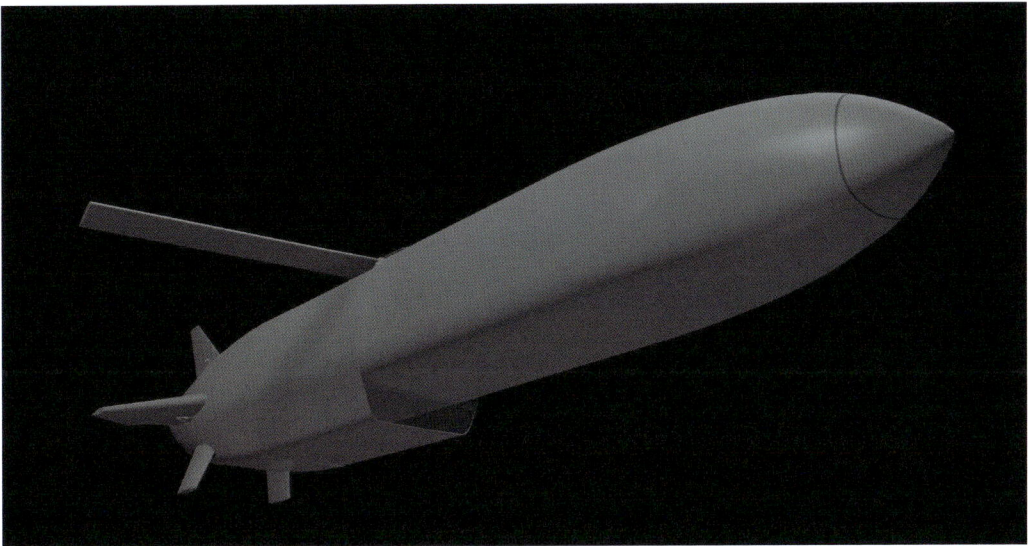

SCALP EG/Storm Shadow with wings in the stowed (folded) position (top) and with wings deployed (bottom). Author/MBDA

Rafale B01 carrying 2 x SCALP EG aerodynamic shapes in company with a Mirage 2000-5 series. Dassault Aviation-F. Robineau

The first phase of the mission-planning regime ensured that the missile navigated to the target with maximum survivability and then entered a robust target acquisition and terminal guidance phase. For complex and pre-determined missions, data would be pre-programed prior to mission commencement. Following an air tasking order, the mission data file would be prepared with the pre-planned data, together with the latest operational intelligence data. On approaching the terminal phase, the missile would initiate a climb manoeuvre, pre-selected during mission planning to obtain the best combination of acquisition probability and lethality against the target. As the missile gained altitude, it would jettison its nose cover, thereby enabling the high resolution imaging infrared sensor to view the target area ahead. The missile image processor compared the actual image features with a reference set of features determined during mission planning. When a feature match was achieved the target would be acquired and the required aim point selection racked and used as the reference for the missile terminal guidance. As the missile closed in on the target, the acquisition process would be repeated with a higher resolution data set to refine the aim point. Tracking would continue against this refined aim point until the precise target location was identified (Harkins, 2004).

SCALP EG carried on the port intermediate wing station of Rafale B01 at Le Bourget in 2001. Author

When engaging hard targets SCALP EG would strike the aim point at the estimated optimum dive angle, selected during mission planning. The precursor charge would perforate the target structure and shallow soil covering, and the follow through penetrator warhead would continue to penetrate to the target to be detonated after a pre-selectable fuse delay. The mission could be aborted if the target identification and acquisition process was unsuccessful. In this case the missile would be pre-programed to fly to a predetermined crash site (Harkins, 2004).

Rafale M02 approaches for landing aboard the *Charles de Gaulle* aircraft carrier, configured with a single SCALP EG on the fuselage centre station. Marine Nationale

Storm Shadow was selected by the British government in July 1996 to meet the RAF CASOM requirement. A development/production contract was awarded in February 1997. In December that year, the French DGA awarded a development contract that would lead to planned production of 500 Scalp EG to equip the Mirage 2000D and Rafale (Harkins, 2004).

Storm Shadow/SCALP EG was acquired by several nations, for which it was integrated on Tornado IDS, Typhoon, Mirage 2000D, Mirage 2000-9 (Mirage 2000-5 MK2) and Rafale. SCALP EG was inducted into French Air Force service on the Mirage 2000D in 2004 and integration on the F2 Standard Rafale M was completed that year following completion of trials with a Rafale M operating from the aircraft carrier *Charles de Gaulle* (MBDA, 2011 & Harkins, 2004).

The first operational use of Storm Shadow occurred during the Anglo-American invasion of Iraq in 2003 (British operation Telic) when British Tornado GR.4 strike aircraft launched 27 missiles against fixed targets. The first operational employment of SCALP EG missiles by France occurred on 24 March 2011 during the intervention of NATO (North Atlantic Treaty Organisation) alliance nations and their proxies in support of rebel forces fighting against forces loyal to the Libyan government during Libyan civil war. On this occasion, SCALP EG missiles were launched from two French Air Force Mirage 2000D, two Rafale B and two French Navy Rafale M operating from the aircraft carrier *Charles de Gaulle*, which was cruising in the Mediterranean Sea. A handful of Storm Shadow missiles were launched from Tornado GR.4 strike aircraft during the Libyan conflict (MBDA, 2011).

SCALP EG carried on the port intermediate wing station of a French Air Force Rafale. MBDA

There were no viable effective defensive capabilities present in any of these conflicts, therefore, whilst qualifying as a quantitative operational employment of SCALP EG/Storm Shadow missiles, it would be hard to qualify the oft quoted statement that the missile and launch platforms had been combat proven. Such statements need to be treated with caution as a true combat proven label can only accepted as qualified if the missile/launch platforms are employed against the most advanced defensive systems available – in 2020 this would include Russian S-400

Triumph long-range (in excess of 400 km) air defence missile systems and perhaps the Russian Pantsir family of short-range missile system. During missile strikes on Syrian targets in April 2018, Syria claimed the destruction of several tens of cruise missiles despite having mostly outdated air defence systems. It is not clear if this claim includes Anglo-French launched Storm Shadow/SCALP EG series missiles. Defensive missile systems are only one aspect of the potential defensive capabilities that would be employed by a technologically advanced adversary, such as the Russian Federation, which has demonstrated widespread advanced capabilities in EW (Electronic Warfare) against GPS guided munitions and aerosol protection of fixed targets against infrared guided threats.

Storm Shadow/SCALP EG Specification – data furnished by MBDA

Weight: 1300 kg
Power plant: Turbojet [TR 60-30]
Length: 5.10 m
Navigation: INS, GPS and Terrain Reference Navigation
Warhead: Blast/penetrator [BROACH unitary warhead]
Range: In excess of 250 km

Rafale B (foreground) configured with 2 x SCALP EG on the inner wing stations. Dassault Aviation-K. Tokunaga

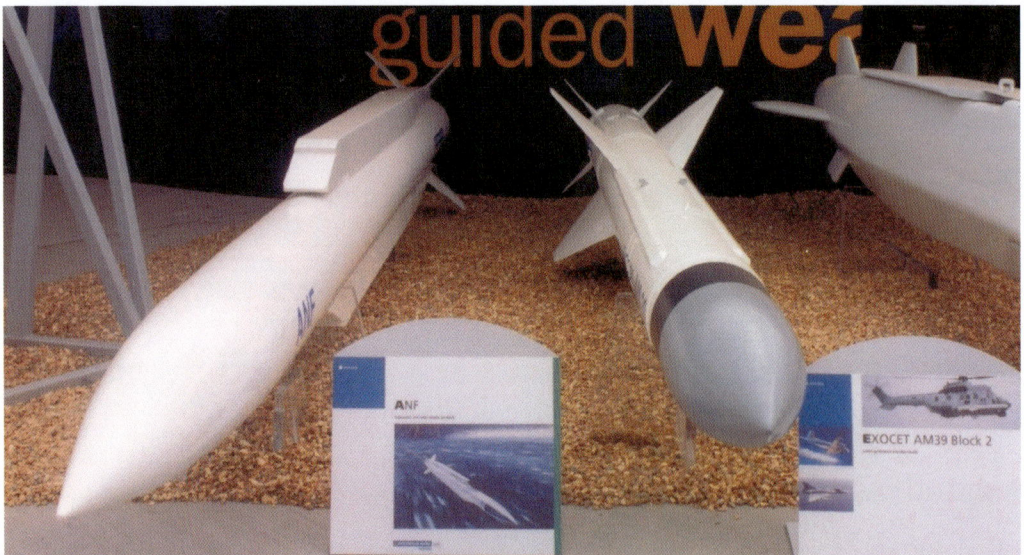

Top: The standard anti-ship weapon in service with the Rafale predecessor, Dassault Super Etendard/(*Modernise***), was the AM 39 Exocet subsonic (sea skimming) cruise missile. Bottom: Mid to late-1990's planning called for the AM 39 to be replaced by the ANF supersonic anti-ship cruise missile (left of image) – ANF was cancelled and the Block 2 AM 39 Exocet (right of image) ordered to arm Rafale M.** Author

EXOCET – For engaging high value surface targets at sea, the Rafale M was armed with the MBDA AM 39 Exocet sea-skimming (several metres above sea surface) air launched anti-ship missile. Exocet – available in air launched (AM 39), sea surface launched (MM 40), submarine launched (SM 39) and BC costal platform launched variants – entered serial production in 1972. Exocet would entered the annals of aviation history as the western world's premier anti-ship missile optimised for sea skimming flight profiles with autonomous radar guidance (MBDA, 2011c). The Dassault Super Etendard/Exocet combination was used to devastating effect by Argentina during the 1982 Falklands conflict, sinking a number of British surface vessels.

Page 151-153: AM 39 Exocet carried on the centre fuselage station of Rafale M1 during integration trials. MBDA

Exocet could be employed in conditions of fair or adverse weather day or night, with a trans-horizon firing capability. Operational features included a low radar signature, sea skimming flight profile, ability to discriminate between multiple target returns, integral ECCM to reduce the potential for electronic interference with the missile flight, on-board RF seeker head activation in late phase of flight to target area (MBDA, 2011c) and high penetration power of the warhead against modern vessels.

Exocet incorporated a number of improvements since introduction in the early 1970's, enabling it to remain viable in the face of modern countermeasures. With the demise of the ANF supersonic anti-ship missile program in 1999, attention turned to capability enhancements of the AM 39. The French DGA authorised development of the Block 2

Mod2 AM 39 in January 2004 (MBDA, 2011c & Harkins, 2004). The Mod2 enhancements digitised the Block 2 AM 39 to bring it up to standards required for operation from $4^{th}+/4^{th}++$ generation airborne platforms, such as Rafale. The development program was completed with the launch of a Block 2 missile from an F3 Standard Rafale in June 2007. This event effectively marked the final validation of the F3 Standard Rafale, clearing the way for service entry of both aircraft and AM 39 missile armament. (MBDA, 2011c).

AM 39 Exocet – data furnished by MBDA, 2011

Weight: 670 kg
Length: 4.69 m
Diameter: 0.35 m
Propulsion: 2 solid-propellant rocket motors (booster and sustainer)
Speed: High subsonic
Range: Up to 70 km, but reduces with decreasing launch altitude
Guidance: Inertial during initial flight phase and active RF in the terminal phase of flight
Steering: Aerodynamic control surfaces
Warhead: Insensitive warhead. Optimised high explosive blast and pre-fragmented effects
Fuse: Impact and proximity

Rafale M02 was employed extensively as a weapon development platform. The aircraft is shown launching a GBU-12 laser guided bomb to clear the weapon for use by the F2 Standard Rafale. DGA-CEV

In the 1990's, the standard French heavy GBL/LGB (*Bombe Guidée Laser*/Laser Guided Bomb) was the MATRA (MBDA) BGL 1000 kg weapon, which was to be carried over to Rafale. Three of these weapons could be carried by Rafale (non-standard), one on the centre fuselage station and one on each of the inboard wing stations (Harkins, 2004).

A fast track program to include a medium weight class precision guided munition capability on the F2 Standard Rafale involved certification for carriage of GBU-12 250 kg class LGB, following trials on Rafale B01 and M02 at the Cazaux test range in South-western France from 2000. A triple-ejector rack, for staggered weapon carriage, was trialled, allowing Rafale to carry six GBU-12, along with a pair of 2000 litre subsonic flight capable external fuel tanks and four MICA air to air missiles (Harkins, 2004).

BANG 125/250 was procured as a domestic alternative to the GBU-12. DGA.

A French solution to provisioning a modern LGB capability of lower mass than the 1000 kg BGL was to be filled by the BANG (*Bombe Aeronavale de Nouvelle Generation*) program. This weapon was developed as a multiple-effects munition, with both fragmentation and penetration warheads. BANG 125 kg and 250 kg class weapons were developed by MBDA, in co-operation with SNPE, for service with the *Aeronavale* Super Etendard (*Modernise*) strike fighter – the first batch of serial produced BANG 125 were delivered for service in September 2000 and later integrated on the F2 and F3 Standard Rafale (Harkins, 2004).

BANG 250 (250 kg class) weapons on Rafale M port intermediate station triple ejector rack. The centre weapon holder of the triple ejector rack is not in use. MBDA

BANG 250 on Rafale M on the deck of the nuclear powered aircraft carrier *Charles de Gaulle.* MBDA

Top: Rafale M12 configured with two x Bang 250 on the starboard intermediate wing station. Bottom: AASM released from Rafale 101. MBDA-Alexandre Paringaux/DGA-CEV-H.P. Grolleau

AASM HAMMER kits can be applied to 125, 250, 500 and 1000 kg class weapons illustrated. MBDA

AASM – Rafale would be armed with the SBU-54 AASM (Armament Air Surface Modulaire) HAMMER (Highly Agile Modular Munition Extended Range), which was developed by Sagem (Safran Group) as a low cost precision guided air launched stand-off weapon. Under a 2008 agreement, MBDA was brought in to market the weapon and participate in future development (MBDA, 2011d & Harkins 2004) – this agreement later became defunct.

The French DGA had authorised procurement of AASM in September 2000. Integration testing on Rafale M commenced in 2003. During this phase, a Rafale M operated from the aircraft carrier *Charles de Gaulle* configured with six AASM. The Rafale M was cleared to land aboard the aircraft carrier at a weight of around 15.7 tonnes, required to allow recovery onto an aircraft carrier deck with six AASM (Harkins, 2004). Further flight test phases were conducted, clearing the AASM for deployment with the Rafale B/C/M.

AASM HAMMER carried on triple ejector rack on the port intermediate wing station of a Rafale. Safran

Treated as a round of ammunition with zero maintenance, thus reducing life cycle costs, AASM HAMMER was integrated on Rafale courtesy of the MIL-STD-1760 interface bus. The AASM HAMMER kit, which could be applied to a number of weapons with warheads for direct impact or airburst, consisted of a guidance kit, which was mated to a standard aerodynamic bomb – typically MK81/82, BLU-111 or BANG. The kit incorporated inertial components and optronics developed by Safran: Hemispheric Resonating Gyro; Inertial GPS hybridisation [hybridisation is a term used in science to denote cross breading of animal or plant species. Its use by Safran in regard to AASM HAMMER is thought to refer to the integration (fusion) of data from inertial and GPS sensors]; Strap-down infrared imagers and associated algorithms. Multiple targets could be engaged by multiple AASM simultaneously in fire and forget launch modes, requiring no further launch platform input as the weapon flew to the target. The weapon possessed a high resistance to the absence of GPS signals and active jamming (Safran Electronics & Defence, 2016).

AASM HAMMER could be launched at a plethora of angles, including wide off-boresight angles, at altitudes ranging from very low to high (this could not exceed the operational launch ceiling of the carrier platform) (Safran Electronics & Defence, 2016). The range extension kit attached to the bomb aft section incorporated a solid-propellant rocket booster and aerodynamic control surfaces designed to aid in generating lift. Target engagement range was stated as 0 km to 70 km – maximum range would depend on launch altitude. A 70 km range would require a medium/high altitude launch. Typical operational range would be in the region of 20 km from medium altitude release. On a low altitude release AASM is credited with a range of 15 km (MBDA, 2011e), but this may be extended as AASM HAMMER development progressed.

The AASM operating parameters fell within the engagement capabilities of modern air defence systems in the class of the Russian Pantsir, particularly when launched from medium altitudes. However, vulnerability would be considerably less than that of an unpowered weapon, such as an LGB unit, and target strike could be accomplished through a terminal phase vertical dive (Safran Electronics & Defence, 2016), further reducing vulnerability to interception in the terminal phase of flight and increasing impact energy.

Top: Rafale M with four AASM. Bottom: French Air Force Rafale B armed with AASM and MICA IR. MBDA/*Armée de l'Air*-C. Amboise

While precision guided weaponry formed the principal armament of all Rafale variants, the extensive stocks of non-guided, non-powered, general purpose weapons could also be cleared for service with the aircraft – non-retarded 125 kg, 250 kg and 400 kg.

5

SERVICE GALLERY

The F2 Standard was employed on operational sorties in Afghanistan from March 2007 (Dassault AR, 2007). Rafale conducted operations in a second deployment to Afghanistan during the period March-June 2008 – the first operational employment of AASM from a Rafale occurred on 18 April that year (Dassault AR, 2008). Rafale operated over Afghanistan in further deployments that ended in 2013. In January that year, Rafale was deployed in Mali under operation Serval – ongoing in 2020 – (one mission involved a Rafale flight covering more than 6000 km in a time of almost ten hours) (Dassault AR, 2013) and, as recounted in the previous chapter, had operated over Libya during the North Atlantic Treaty Organisation air campaign against Libyan loyalist forces during the Libyan civil war in 2011. In 2014, France deployed Rafale in support of coalition efforts to assist Iraqi forces fighting against ISIL/Islamic State of Iraq and the Levant, the operation extending to missions over Syria from 2015 (Dassault AR, 2015 & Dassault AR, 2014).

As briefly touched upon in the previous chapter, it is oft stated for Rafale, as for other 4th+ generation combat aircraft, that they had been tried and tested under combat conditions. A more accurate description would be that they have been tested under operational conditions, but not against the most advanced air threats currently available. The combat proven label would be difficult to reconcile with the facts of the operations. It is more appropriate to state that Rafale had proven strike and reconnaissance capability in operations. However, Rafale, as is the case with other airborne platforms of its generation, such as Eurofighter Typhoon, have never operated against a modern airborne or surface to air threat environment. Over Afghanistan, Iraq, Mali, The Central African Republic and Syria, Rafale faced no airborne threat whatsoever and encountered no credible surface to air threat. Over Syria, Rafale operations were often monitored by Russian Sukhoi Su-35S/30SM 4++/4+ generation multifunctional fighter aircraft, but the de-confliction measures put in-place ensured that only detection and identification functions were conducted by all parties. In regard to advanced capability Russian air defence systems deployed in Syria, coalition air assets avoided, where possible, coming into areas actively covered by such systems and were merely monitored by the Russian systems to ensure no threat was present. In the operations over Libya, the defensive capability – airborne and ground based – fielded by Libyan loyalist forces was outdated – 1970's/1980's vintage – posing no credible threat to coalition tactical air operations conducted by 4+/4++ generation combat aircraft in the class of Rafale. The electronic counter measures environment in all these operational theatres was either non-existent or obsolete. In this regard we should observe caution when assessing the 'combat proven' (designer/operators) epithet.

F2 Standard Rafale Marine, M12, operating (together with M13) from the USS *Enterprise* **(CVN 65) cruising off Cannes on 23 July 2007.** USN

French Rafale B operating over Afghanistan during Operation Serpentaire armed with 4 x AASM – note the absence of air to air missile armament as the aircraft faced no air defence threat. *Armée de l'Air*

Top: Rafale B during operation Harmattan (French participation in NATO campaign against Libyan loyalist forces) in 2011. Bottom: Rafale B approaches the air refuelling tanker boom trailing a drogue basket during operation Harmattan in 2011. *Armée de l'Air/Armée de l'Air*-A Jeuland

Rafale C (top) and Rafale B/C (bottom) during operation Harmattan in 2011.
Armée de l'Air-C. Amboise/*Armée de l'Air*-R. Nicolas-Nelson

Rafale C during operation Harmattan configured for an air defence role (top) and armed with AASM for air to surface operations and air to air missiles for self defence (bottom). *Armée de l'Air*-R. Nicolas-Nelson/*Armée de l'Air*

Rafale B armed with AASM and MICA IR during operation Harmattan. *Armée de l'Air*-A. Jeuland/*Armée de l'Air*

Top: Rafale B take-off during operation Harmattan armed with AASM and MICA IR. Bottom: Rafale B over Mali during operation Serval, configured with 6 x GBU-12 laser guided bombs, 3 x 2000 litre external fuel tanks and a DAMOCLES pod. *Armée de l'Air*-W. Collet/*Armée de l'Air*-A. Jeuland

Two Rafale during operation Serval configured with four x AASM guided air to surface munitions, three 2000 litre external fuel tanks and a DAMOCLES pod – note the absence of air to air missile armament as the aircraft faced no air defence threat. *Armée de l'Air*

F2 Standard Rafale M's conduct touch and go on CVN 71 (USS *Theodore Roosevelt*) nuclear powered aircraft carrier in 2008 (top) and the USS *John C. Stennis* nuclear powered aircraft carrier in 2007 (bottom). USN

French Air Force Rafale are periodically adorned in special livery in deference to **NATO** squadrons with a reference to Tigers in their respective lineage.
Dassault Aviation

Top: French Rafale C flies in formation with a USAF F-15C Eagle during a training exercise in Southwest Asia. Bottom: Rafale M in clean configuration engages afterburner on the two x M88-2 engines at Le Bourget in June 2005. USAF/Safran-Frederic Lert

Top: Rafale M takes the wire as it comes aboard the *Charles de Gaulle* during the 8th test campaign in May 2012. Bottom: Rafale M during trials, configured with **MICA EM, MICA IR** and a single **1250** litre external fuel tank on the centre fuselage station. Dassault Aviation-S. Rande/MBDA

Two Rafale B (top) and one Rafale B and one Rafale C (bottom). *Armée de l'Air*-A. Jeuland/Dassault Aviation

In 2020, the Rafale program was centred on delivery of aircraft to export customers – a single-seat Indian Air Force Rafale is delivered to Ambala air base for No.17 Squadron 'Golden Arrows' in summer 2020 (top) – and the update of F3 Standard to F3-R Standard for French domestic operators (bottom). Dassault Aviation

The combination of F3 Standard Rafale and the forward deploy potential of the *Charles de Gaulle* nuclear powered aircraft carrier bestow upon France a quasi-strategic strike power projection capability. That said, the aircraft carrier would be extremely vulnerable to the new generation supersonic/hypersonic anti-ship missiles fielded by technologically advanced nations. Dassault Aviation/DGA/Marine Nationale

6

FUTURE DEVELOPMENT

Current (2020) planning calls for the Rafale to retain its position as the premier French domestic airborne combat platform until around 2040 (Dassault, 2020). To this end, development of the Rafale platform was ongoing, with the F4 Standard progressing toward planned service release in 2024, and initial studies for the F5 Standard was planned to formally commence in 2020 (Dassault AR, 2019).

There were no details on the specifics of the F5 Standard available in mid-2020, but this could potentially draw on technology developed under the NGF (Next Generation Fighter), studied under the FCAS (Future Combat Air System) research effort – Dassault was designated industrial leader of the NGF (Next Generation Fighter) program (Dassault AR, 2019).

In the second decade of the twenty first century France had been studying the potential for UAV/UCAV (Uninhabited Air Vehicle/Uninhabited Combat Air Vehicle) operations in concert with manned aircraft operations. This was conducted in cooperation between Dassault Aviation and BAE Systems under the guise of the FCAS studies. During 2016, a Rafale M and the nEURon UCAV demonstrator operated with the *Charles de Gaulle* aircraft carrier on trials (Dassault AR, 2016), building on previous trials that had effectively commenced when a Rafale flew in formation with nEURon on that platforms maiden flight, conducted on 1 December 2012 (Dassault AR, 2012). In 2017, the FCAS concept, which was in effect a planned multitude of interlinked vehicle/weapons centred on an omnirole combat aircraft platform, was scheduled for introduction in 2040 (Dassault AR, 2017).

In 2016 and 2017, studies continued into the feasibility of a small airborne space launcher carried by Rafale, or a Dassault Falcon business class passenger jet, on behalf of CNES (French Space Agency). This concept involved the use of a partially reusable launch vehicle capable of placing small satellites into low-Earth orbit (Dassault AR, 2016 & Dassault AR, 2017). In 2020, the future of this program was unclear in a competitive market that included a number of potential solutions to air launch of small payloads into Earth orbit. What was clear in 2020 was that Rafale was firmly established as the premier combat aircraft platform in French domestic service and was in service with three export nations, with a service life expected to extend considerably beyond the 2040 date set for acquisition of the NGF to be developed under the auspices of the FCAS.

Artist depiction of Rafale operating with nEURon uninhabited combat air vehicles. Rafale may operate alongside uninhabited aircraft in the coming decades. Dassault Aviation

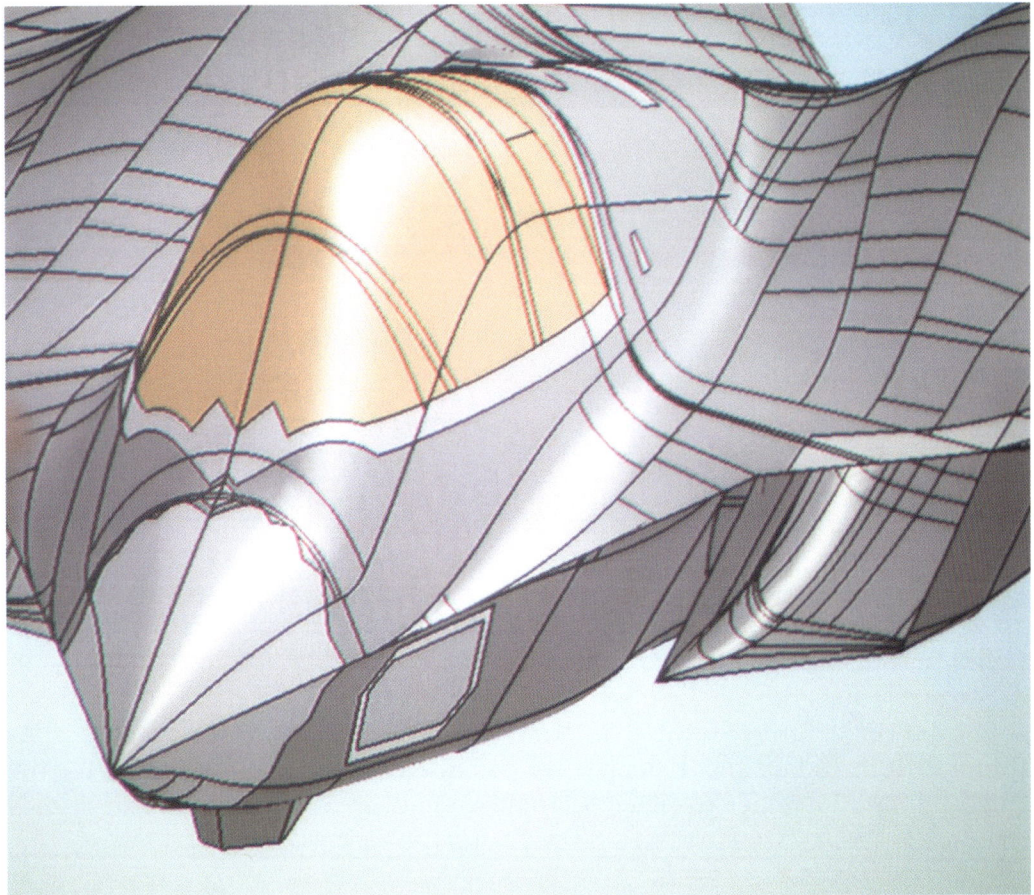

Previous page top: Rafale M operating with the nEURon demonstrator. Previous page bottom: CAD drawing of a future fighter concept drawing on Rafale heritage. Top: The NGF was born from the FCAS studies conducted in the second decade of the twenty first century to research technologies applicable to a future combat aircraft to replace Rafale from around 2040. Bottom: Both Rafale and Falcon were considered as carrier platforms for the small satellite launcher to place a small payload in low Earth orbit. Dassault Aviation-A. Pechhi/Dassault Aviation-A. Daste/Dassault Aviation-V. Almansa

GLOSSARY

2D	Two Dimensional
3D	Three Dimensional
AASM HAMMER	Armament Air Sol Modulaire (Armament Air to Surface Modular) Highly Agile Modular Munition Extended Range
ACA	Agile Combat Aircraft
ACE	Avion de Combat European
ACT	Avion de Combat Tactique
ACX	Avion de Combat Experimental
AESA	Active Electronically Scanned Array
ANF	New Generation Anti-Ship Missile
APACHE	Arme Propulsée À Charges Éjectables
AREOS	Airborne Reconnaissance Observation System
ASLP	Air Sol Longue Portée
ASMP	Air-Sol Moyenne Portée
ASMPA	Air-Sol Moyenne Portée Amélioré
AST	Air Staff Target
BAC	British Aircraft Corporation
BAe	British Aerospace
BAE	British Aerospace (SYSTEMS)
BANG	Bombe Aeronavale de Nouvelle Generation
BROACH	Bomb Royal Ordnance Augmented Charge
BVR	Beyond Visual Range
BVRAAM	Beyond Visual Range Air to Air Missile
C	Celsius
C4ISR	Command Control Communication Computer Intelligence Surveillance Reconnaissance
CAD	Computer Aided Drawing
CASOM	Conventionally Armed Stand-Off Missile
CEA	Commissariat à l'énergie Atomique
CEAM	Centre d'Expérimentation Aérienne Militaire
CEV	Centre d'Essais en Vol
CFC	Carbon Fibre Composite
COTS	Commercial (Common) off The Shelf
CTBTO	Comprehensive Nuclear Test Ban Treaty Organisation
CVN	Aircraft Carrier Nuclear Powered
DGA	Délégué Général pour l'armament
DRAL	Dassault Reliance Aerospace Limited
EAP	Experimental Aircraft Program
EC	Escadron de Chasse
ECA	European Combat Aircraft
ECCM	Electronic Counter Counter Measures
ECF	European Combat Fighter

EFA	European Fighter Aircraft
EG	Emploi Général (General Purpose)
ESA	Electronically Scanned Array
ESR	European Staff Requirement
EW	Electronic Warfare
F	Fahrenheit
FADEC	Full Authority Digital Engine Control Unit
FAF	French Air Force
FBW	Fly By Wire
FCAS	Future Combat Air System
FCS	Flight Control System
FEFA	Future European Fighter Aircraft
FG	Fighter Ground attack
FGR	Fighter Ground attack Reconnaissance
FLIR	Forward Looking Infrared
FNS	French Naval Ship
FSD	Full Scale Development
FSO	Front Sector Optronics
ft.	Foot (feet) – unit of measurement
g	Gravity (1 g = 1 x Earth gravity)
GBL	Bombe Guidée Laser
GE	General Electric
HD	High Definition
HL	Heads Level
HP	High Pressure
HOTAS	Hands On Throttle And Stick
HUD	Heads Up Display
IDS	Interdiction Strike
IFF	Identification Friend or Foe
II	Roman numeral number two
III	Roman numeral number three
IIR	Imaging Infrared
IMINT	Image Intelligence
INS/GPS	Inertial Navigation System/Global Positioning System
INU	Inertial Navigation Unit
IR	Infrared
IR/EM/EO	Infrared/Electromagnetic/Electro-optical
IRST	Infrared Search & Track
IV	Roman numeral number four
kg	Kilogram
kgf	Kilogram force – unit of thrust
kg/kgf/h	Kilogram per kilogram force per hour
Kiloton	1 kiloton = 1000 tons of TNT equivalent explosive force
km/h	Kilometers per hour
kN	Kilonewton

Knot	Nautical Miles Per Hour
lb.	Pound – unit of weight
lb./lbf./h	Pound/per pound force/per hour
lbf.	Pound/force – unit of thrust
LCA	Light Combat Aircraft
LGB	Laser Guided Bomb
LP	Low Pressure
LRU	Line Replaceable Unit
m	Metre
Mach	1 Mach = the speed of sound (this varies with altitude)
MAW	Modular Abstandswaffe
MBB	Messerschmitt-Bölkow-Blohm
MBDA	Matra British Aerospace Dynamics Alenia
MDPU	Modular Data Processing Unit
MICA EM	Missile d'Interception de Combat et d' Autodéfence (radar guided)
MICA IR	Missile d'Interception de Combat et d' Autodéfence (infrared guided)
mm	Millimetre
MMI	Man Machine Interface
MRCA	Multi-Role Combat Aircraft
MWS	Missile Warning System
m/s	Metres per second
NAS	Naval Air Station
NATO	North Atlantic Treaty Organisation
NG	Next Generation
NGF	Next Generation Fighter
OSF	Optronique Secteur Frontal
RACAAS	*Radar de Combat Aéiren et d'Ataque au Sol*
RAF	Royal Air Force
RBE2	Radar a Balayage Electronic 2 plans
RBG	Radar du Bord du GIE
RF	Radio Frequency
ROVER	Remotely Operated Video Enhanced Receiver
SAR	Synthetic Aperture Radar
SBAC	Society of British Aerospace Companies
SEMMB	Consortium of Safran and Martin Baker France
SEPECAT	Societe Europeene de Production de Avion de Ecole de Combat et de' Appuie Tactique
SIRPA Air	Ministére des Armées/Ministry of the Armed Forces
SPECTRA	Self-Protection Equipment to Counter Threats for Rafale Aircraft
SR(A)	Staff Requirement (Air)
SRU	Shop (Workshop) Replaceable Unit
STOL	Short Take-Off and Landing

STOVL	Short Take-Off and Vertical Landing
TALIOS	Targeting Long-range Identification System
TCO	Total Cost of Ownership
TERPROM	Terrain Profile Matching
TKF	Taktisches Kampfflugeuz
TNT	Trinitrotoluene – a high explosive chemical formation
TV	Television
T/R	Transmit/Receive
UAE	United Arab Emirates
UAV	Uninhabited Air Vehicle
UCAV	Uninhabited Combat Air Vehicle
UK	United Kingdom
US	United States
US DoD	United States Department of Defence
USA	United States of America
USAF	United States Air Force
USS	United States Ship
VMTWS	Versatile Multi target Track While Scan
μm	Micrometre (one millionth of one metre)
%	Percentage
x	Times, multiplication
~	Approximately equal to (can also be used to mean asymptotically equal)
°	Degree(s)

BIBLIOGRAPHY

CTBTO (2011) 'Report of France last nuclear test, conducted on 27 January 1996', Comprehensive Nuclear Test Ban Treaty Organisation

Dassault Aviation (2005) '2005 Annual Report', Dassault Aviation, France

Dassault Aviation (2006) '2006 Annual Report', Dassault Aviation, France

Dassault Aviation (2007) '2007 Annual Report', Dassault Aviation, France

Dassault Aviation (2008) '2008 Annual Report', Dassault Aviation, France

Dassault Aviation (2009) '2009 Annual Report', Dassault Aviation, France

Dassault Aviation (2010) '2010 Annual Report', Dassault Aviation, France

Dassault Aviation (2011) '2011 Annual Report', Dassault Aviation, France

Dassault Aviation (2012) '2012 Annual Report', Dassault Aviation, France

Dassault Aviation (2013) '2013 Annual Report', Dassault Aviation, France

Dassault Aviation (2014) '2014 Annual Report', Dassault Aviation, France

Dassault Aviation (2015) '2015 Annual Report', Dassault Aviation, France

Dassault Aviation (2016) '2016 Annual Report', Dassault Aviation, France

Dassault Aviation (2017) '2017 Annual Report', Dassault Aviation, France

Dassault Aviation (2018) '2018 Annual Report', Dassault Aviation, France

Dassault Aviation (2019) '2019 Annual Report', Dassault Aviation, France

Dassault Aviation (2007) 'Rafale' [Program Information], Dassault Aviation, France

Dassault Aviation (2020) 'Rafale' [Program Information], Dassault Aviation, France

Dassault Aviation (2017) 'Rafale Development History', Dassault Aviation

Dassault Aviation (2019) 'NGF [Next Generation Fighter]' [Backgrounder], Dassault Aviation

Dassault Aviation (undated) 'Safran's contribution to the Rafale', Dassault Aviation

Harkins, H. (1997) 'Eurofighter 2000, Europe's Combat Aircraft for the New Millennium', Midland Publishing (Ian Allan Publishing), United Kingdom

Harkins, H. (2004) 'Dassault Rafale, the Gallic Squall', Centurion Publishing, United Kingdom

Harkins, H. (2004) 'Eurofighter Typhoon, Storm over Europe', Centurion Publishing, United Kingdom

Harkins, H. (2013) 'Eurofighter Typhoon, Storm over Europe', 2nd Edition, Centurion Publishing, United Kingdom

JEWC/MBDA (undated) 'SPECTRA on board the Rafale', Joint Electronic Warfare Centre/MATRA British Aerospace Dynamics Alenia

MBDA (2011) 'AASM' [Backgrounder], MBDA Missile Systems

MBDA (2015) 'ASMPA Air-To-Ground Missile, Medium Range, Enhanced' Product characteristics, MBDA France

MBDA (2011) 'BANG, A New Generation of Multi-Purpose Insensitive Bombs', MBDA Missile Systems

MBDA (2015) 'BANG, A New Generation of Multi-Purpose Insensitive Bombs', MBDA Missile Systems

MBDA (2018) 'BANG, A New Generation of Multi-Purpose Insensitive Bombs', MBDA Missile Systems

MBDA (2018) 'DDM-NG Missile Warning System for Rafale', MBDA Missile Systems

MBDA (2011) 'EXOCET AM 39 Air Launched Anti-Ship Missile', Product characteristics, MBDA France

MBDA (2011) 'EXOCET' [Backgrounder], MBDA Missile Systems

MBDA (2011) 'EXOCET', Press release, MBDA Missile Systems, June 2011

MBDA (2018) 'EXOCET AM 39 Air Launched Anti-Ship Missile', Product characteristics, MBDA France

MBDA (2019) 'Germany orders more Meteor Missiles', Press release, MBDA Missile Systems

MBDA (2004) 'Gripen Trials Success Marks Next Milestone for Meteor', Press release, 22 April 2004, MBDA Missile Systems

MBDA (2018) 'MBDA to develop the next generation of the MICA missile', Press release, 09/11/2018, MBDA Missile Systems

MBDA (2007) 'Meteor High Altitude Firing Marks Next Test Success', Press release, 23 April 2007, MBDA Missile Systems

MBDA (2011) 'Meteor Beyond Visual Range Air-to-Air Missile (BVRAAM)', Product characteristics, MBDA United Kingdom

MBDA (2011) 'Meteor: The Background Information, MBDA Missile Systems

MBDA (2012) 'MBDA's Meteor Firings Conclude with Lethal Display', Press release, 9 July 2012, MBDA Missile Systems

MBDA (2013) 'Meteor e-Catalogue', MBDA

MBDA (2013) 'Meteor: The Background Environment, MBDA Missile Systems

MBDA (2015) 'Meteor Beyond Visual Range Air-to-Air Missile (BVRAAM)', Product characteristics, MBDA United Kingdom

MBDA (2018) 'Meteor Beyond Visual Range Air-to-Air Missile (BVRAAM)', Product characteristics, MBDA United Kingdom

MBDA (2011) 'MICA Multi-Mission Air-to-Air Missile System', Product characteristics, MBDA Missile Systems

MBDA (2011) 'MICA (E,) RF/MICA IR' [Backgrounder], MBDA Missile Systems

MBDA (2015) 'SPECTRA Integrated Self-Protection System for the Rafale', MBDA Missile Systems

MBDA (2011) 'Storm Shadow/SCALP' [Backgrounder], MBDA Missile Systems

MBDA (2011) 'Storm Shadow SCALP: Conventionally Armed Long Range Deep Strike Weapon', MBDA Missile Systems, United Kingdom

MBDA (2017) 'Storm Shadow SCALP: Conventionally Armed Long Range Deep Strike Weapon', MBDA Missile Systems, France/United Kingdom

MBDA (2019) 'Storm Shadow SCALP: Conventionally Armed Long Range Deep Strike Weapon', MBDA Missile Systems, United Kingdom

MBDA/Safran (2011) 'AASM Modular Air-to-Ground Weapon, MBDA Missile Systems/Sagem Défense Sécurité-Safran Group, France

Safran (Undated) '2 Seconds to save a life', Safran, France

Safran (2016) 'AASM HAMMER Highly Agile Modular Munition Extended Range', Safran Electronics and Defense, France

Thales Optronique (2013) 'Front Sector Optronics, FSO', Technical Characteristics,

Thales Group, France

Thales Optronique SAS (2014) 'DAMOCLES Multi-function targeting pod', Airborne Optronics, Technical Characteristics, Thales Group, France

Thales Optronique SAS (2016) 'Airborne Reconnaissance Observation System', Airborne Optronics, Technical Characteristics, Thales Group, France

Thales Optronique SAS (2016) 'DAMOCLES Multi-function targeting pod', Airborne Optronics, Technical Characteristics, Thales Group, France

Thales las France SAS (2019) 'TALIOS New generation Omnirole Pod', Technical Characteristics, Thales Group, France

Thales Systémes Aéroportés SAS (2013) 'Thales on board the Rafale', Thales Group, France

Thales Systémes Aéroportés (2013) 'AESA RBE2 Active Electronically Scanned Array Radar', Thales Group, France

Thales (2020) 'Airborne Optronics', Thales Group

Thales (undated) 'FSO: Front Sector Optronics', Technical Characteristics, Thales Group, France

ABOUT THE AUTHOR

Hugh Harkins FRAS, MIstP, MRAeS is a physicist/historian and author with an extensive research/study background in aeronautic, astronautic, astrophysics, geophysics, nautical and the wider scientific, technical and historical fields. He is also involved in research in the field of Scottish history, which formed a significant element of dual undergraduate degrees. Hugh has published in excess of sixty books, non-fiction and fiction, writing under his given name as well as utilising several pseudonyms. He has also written for several international magazines, whilst his work has been used as reference for many other projects, ranging from the aviation industry, international news corporations and film media to encyclopaedias, museum exhibits and the computer gaming industry. Hugh an elected member of the Institute of Physics and Royal Aeronautical Society and is an elected Fellow of the Royal Astronomical Society. He currently resides in his native Scotland. Other titles by the author include:

X-35 – Progenitor to the F-35 Lightning II
X-32 - The Boeing Joint Strike Fighter
Boeing X-36 Tailless Agility Flight Research Aircraft
XF-103 – Mach 3 Stratospheric Interceptor Concept
North American F-108 Rapier - Mach 3 Interceptor
Convair YB-60 - Fort Worth Overcast
Russia's Coastal Missile Shield - Bal-E & Bastion Mobile Coastal Cruise Missile Complexes
Iskander - Mobile Tactical Aero-Ballistic/Cruise Missile Complex
Orbital/Fractional Orbit Bombardment System - The Soviet Globalnaya Raketa
Counter-Space Defence Co-Orbital Satellite Fighter
Russia's Strategic Missile Carrier/Bomber Roadmap 2018-2040 – PAK DA, Tu-160M2, Tu-95MSM
& Tu-22M3M
Sukhoi T-50/PAK FA - Russia's 5th Generation 'Stealth' Fighter
Sukhoi Su-35S 'Flanker' E - Russia's 4++ Generation Super-Manoeuvrability Fighter
Sukhoi Su-30MKK/MK2/M2 - Russo Kitashiy Striker from Amur
MiG-35/D 'Fulcrum' F – Towards the Fifth Generation
Air War over Syria, Tu-160, Tu-95MS & Tu-22M3 - Cruise Missile and Bombing Strikes on Syria,
November 2015-February 2016
Sukhoi Su-27SM(3)/SKM
Russian/Soviet Aircraft Carrier & Carrier Aviation Design & Evolution Volume 1 -
Seaplane Carriers, Project 71/72, Graf Zeppelin, Project 1123 ASW Cruiser & Project 1143-1143.4
Heavy Aircraft Carrying Cruiser
Soviet Mixed Power Experimental Fighter Aircraft – Piston-Liquid Propellant Rocket Engine/Piston-
Ramjet/Piston-Pulsejet & Piston-Compressor Jet Engine Designs of the 1940's
Raid on the Forth - The First German Air Raid on Great Britain in World War II
Light Battle Cruisers and the Second Battle of Heligoland Bight
Into The Cauldron - The Lancaster MK.I Daylight Raid on Augsburg
Hurricane IIB Combat Log - 151 Wing RAF, North Russia 1941
RAF Meteor Jet Fighters in World War II, an Operational Log
Typhoon IA/B Combat Log - Operation Jubilee, August 1942
Defiant MK.I Combat Log - Fighter Command, May-September 1940
Blenheim MK.IF Combat Log - Fighter Command Day Fighter Sweeps/Night
Interceptions, September 1939 - June 1940
Fortress MK.I Combat Log - Bomber Command High Altitude Bombing Operations, July-
September1941
Light Battle Cruisers and the Second Battle of Heligoland Bight

Printed in Great Britain
by Amazon